GOLF

SKILLS AND TECHNIQUES

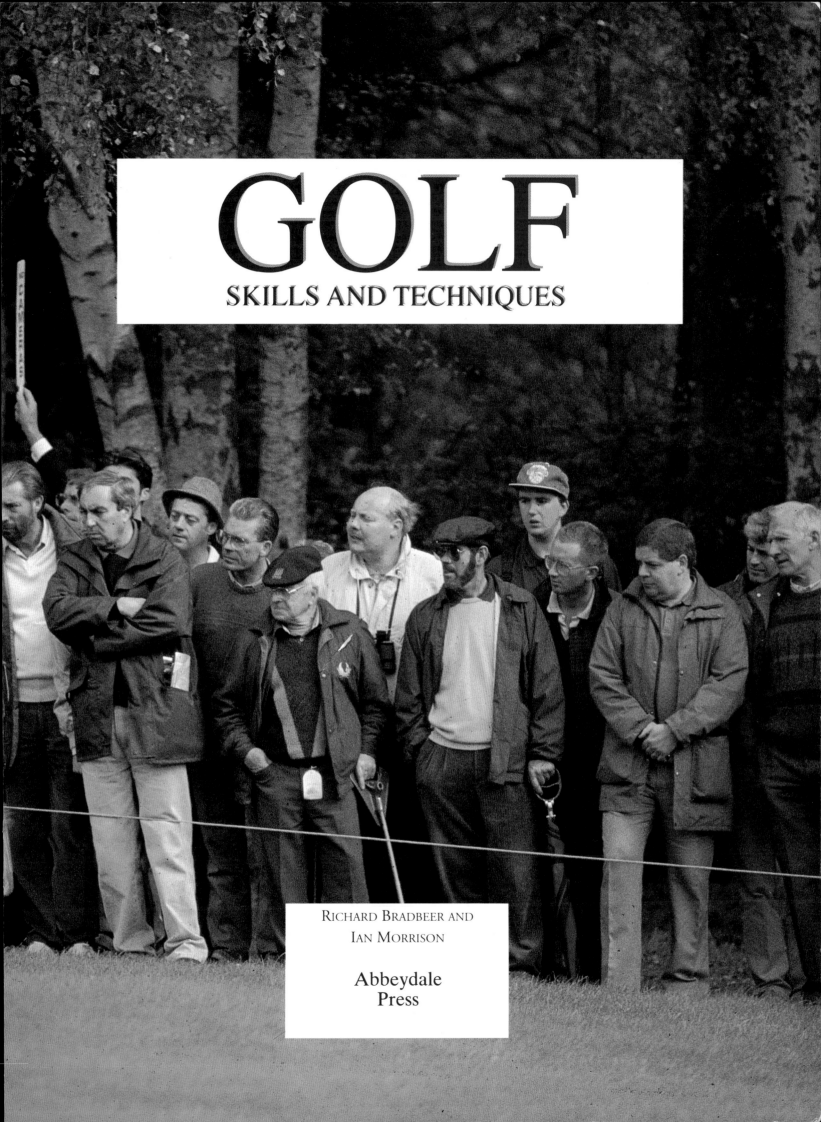

GOLF
SKILLS AND TECHNIQUES

RICHARD BRADBEER AND
IAN MORRISON

Abbeydale
Press

This edition published in 2002 by
Abbeydale Press
Desford Road, Enderby,
Leicester LE19 4AD
England

Typeset by MC Typeset Limited
Printed and bound in Singapore
by Star Standard Industries

© Bookmart Limited 1996

ISBN 1-86147-068-1

Editorial Director: Joanna Lorenz
Art Director: Tony Paine
Designer: Barry Jordan
Photographer: Ian Howes

Page one:
Payne Stewart.

Previous page:
Ian Woosnam.

ACKNOWLEDGMENTS

The authors and publishers would like to thank the Penina
Hotel and Golf Course in Portugal for their hospitality during
the location photography, and Clare Seddon and Michael
Hobbs for their assistance.

The publishers and authors would also like to thank the
Michael Hobbs Golf Collection for the pictures appearing on
pages 2, 5 (below), 6–8, 17 (below), 18, 28–30, 37, 38, 43, 48,
49, 80, 123, 135 and 147; Peter Dazeley for the pictures
appearing on pages 1, 5 (above), 53, 84, 91, 103 and 114; and
Phil Sheldon for pages 19, 65 and 115.

PUBLISHER'S NOTE

The publishers would like to point out that the instructions in
this book assume that the player is right-handed. If you are a
left-handed player you should reverse the instructions.

CONTENTS

PLAYING THE GAME

Nick Faldo.

Amy Alcott.

RULES AND ETIQUETTE

PLAYING THE GAME

INTRODUCTION

One of the truly great things about the game of golf is that it can be played by men and women of all ages and from all walks of life. It is a game that requires concentration with both the body and the mind, but the rewards are so great that it makes all of the effort worthwhile.

EQUIPMENT

CLUBS

Golf clubs can now be purchased at many outlets, but it is always best to deal with one that is qualified to give you the correct advice and one you can contact should you have any problems. Value for money does not always mean buying the cheapest clubs and if you deal with the known brands, you will be able to get a comprehensive back-up service.

CLUBS

Top: The current trend is for clubheads with a cavity back. They claim to give a greater sweet spot to strike the ball with. Bottom: A blade-type clubhead.

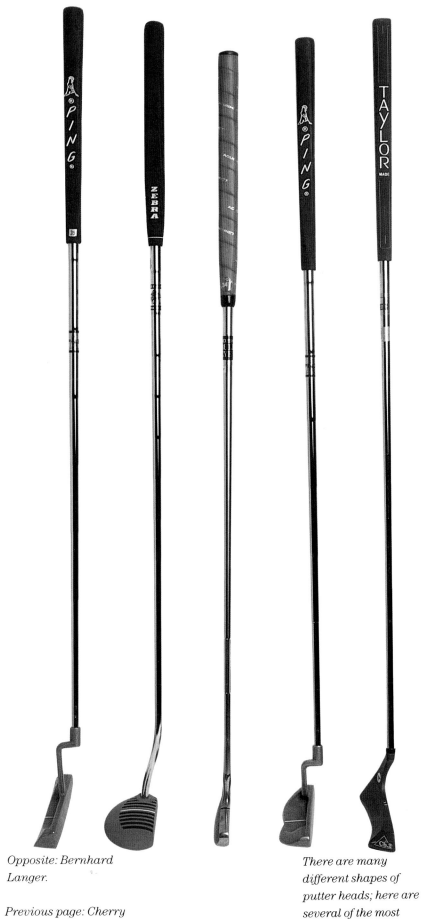

Opposite: Bernhard Langer.

Previous page: Cherry Hills.

There are many different shapes of putter heads; here are several of the most popular.

A HALF-SET FOR BEGINNERS

When you first start playing golf it is not necessary to buy all fourteen clubs, seven is sufficient for any new player. A good combination to have would be a 3-wood, 3-, 5-, 7-, 9-irons, a sand wedge and a putter. Alternatively, you could select a 3- and 5-wood, 4-, 6- and 8-irons, a sand wedge and a putter. When buying your first set of clubs it is best to seek the advice of a PGA Professional, as they will be able to help you choose the clubs best suited to your build and physical strength.

SHAFTS

There are a few points to bear in mind when you purchase new or second-hand clubs. There are many shafts on the market and they can vary a great deal in flex, weight and type. The most flexible shafts 'L' are generally used for ladies' golf clubs, 'R' are used by the majority of men and 'S' by stronger players. Always check that the shaft is correct for your requirements.

A half-set of clubs suitable for a beginner comprising a 3-wood, 3-, 5-, 7-, and 9-irons, a sand wedge and putter.

Two hand-made wooden golf clubs.

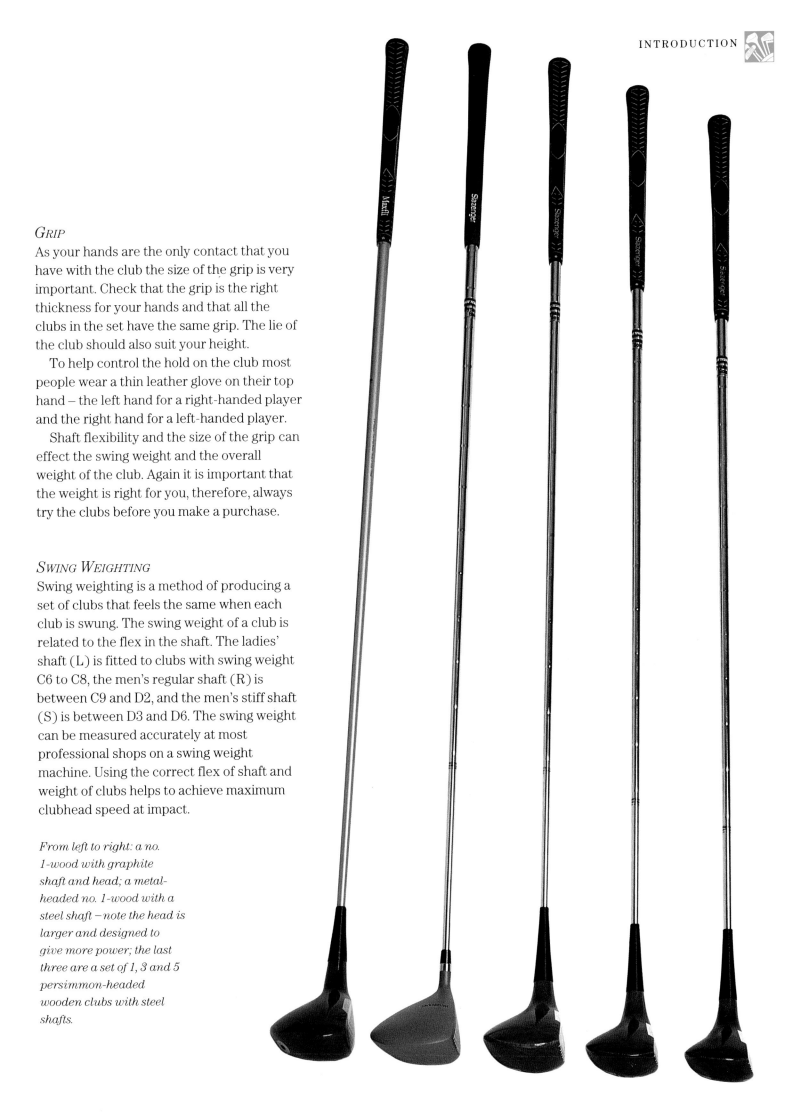

GRIP

As your hands are the only contact that you have with the club the size of the grip is very important. Check that the grip is the right thickness for your hands and that all the clubs in the set have the same grip. The lie of the club should also suit your height.

To help control the hold on the club most people wear a thin leather glove on their top hand – the left hand for a right-handed player and the right hand for a left-handed player.

Shaft flexibility and the size of the grip can effect the swing weight and the overall weight of the club. Again it is important that the weight is right for you, therefore, always try the clubs before you make a purchase.

SWING WEIGHTING

Swing weighting is a method of producing a set of clubs that feels the same when each club is swung. The swing weight of a club is related to the flex in the shaft. The ladies' shaft (L) is fitted to clubs with swing weight C6 to C8, the men's regular shaft (R) is between C9 and D2, and the men's stiff shaft (S) is between D3 and D6. The swing weight can be measured accurately at most professional shops on a swing weight machine. Using the correct flex of shaft and weight of clubs helps to achieve maximum clubhead speed at impact.

From left to right: a no. 1-wood with graphite shaft and head; a metal-headed no. 1-wood with a steel shaft – note the head is larger and designed to give more power; the last three are a set of 1, 3 and 5 persimmon-headed wooden clubs with steel shafts.

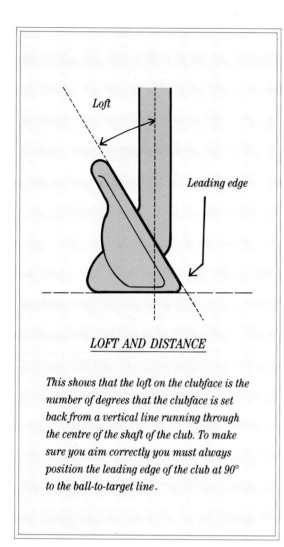

LOFT AND DISTANCE

This shows that the loft on the clubface is the number of degrees that the clubface is set back from a vertical line running through the centre of the shaft of the club. To make sure you aim correctly you must always position the leading edge of the club at 90° to the ball-to-target line.

IRONS	LOFT	LENGTH OF SHAFT In (mm)	APPROX. DISTANCE Yd (ms)
2	18°	38½ (978)	190 (174)
3	22°	38 (965)	180 (165)
4	26°	37½ (953)	170 (155)
5	30°	37 (940)	160 (146)
6	34°	36½ (927)	150 (137)
7	38°	36 (914)	140 (128)
8	42°	35½ (902)	130 (119)
9	46°	35 (889)	120 (110)
Pitching wedge	52°	35 (889)	100 (91)
Sand wedge	58°	35 (889)	80 (73)
WOODS			
1	12°	43 (1092)	240 (219)
2	16°	42½ (1080)	220 (201)
3	20°	42 (1066)	200 (183)
4	24°	41½ (1054)	180 (165)
5	28°	41 (1040)	170 (155)

LOFT AND DISTANCE

You are allowed to have fourteen clubs in your bag when playing golf. Each club serves a different purpose and is used for hitting different distances. This is determined by the loft on the clubface. The lower the number on the sole of the club the less the loft on the face. As the number of each club increases the loft goes up 4°, and the length of the shaft decreases by ½in (12.5mm)

The longest club has less loft, it can therefore hit the ball further, and this is helped by the longer shaft which gives a greater radius to the swing.

As the metal-headed wood gets smaller it also becomes shallower in the face, enabling the clubhead to fit in behind the ball when it is lying on the fairway or rough.

The head on the irons gets larger with a deeper face as the irons get shorter. This enables the club to hit the ball up in the air.

A set of clubs consisting of three metal-headed woods (nos. 1, 3 and 5), and nine irons (nos. 3 to 9, a wedge and a sand wedge) With the addition of a putter and either another wood or iron they would make up the club set.

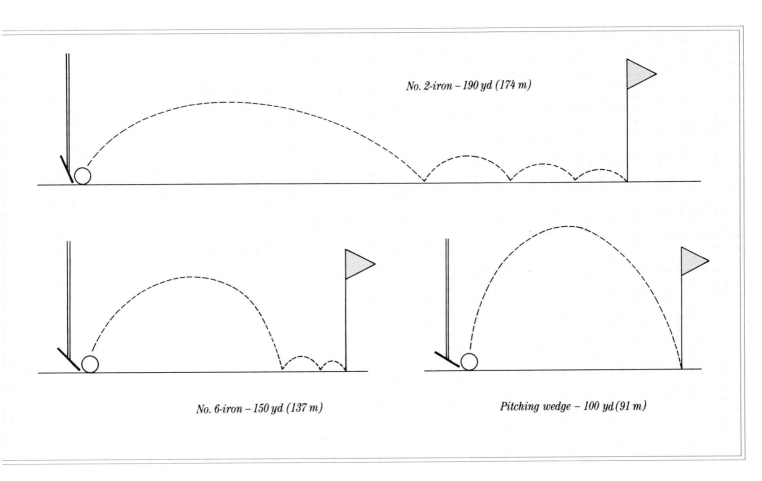

No. 2-iron – 190 yd (174 m)

No. 6-iron – 150 yd (137 m)

Pitching wedge – 100 yd (91 m)

THE GOLF BALL

Golf balls used all over the world are now of universal size – 1.68in (42.5mm) in diameter and weighing 1.62oz (46g). There are basically three types of balls on the market, each varying in the materials used and their performance and durability.

BALATA

Balata is the first choice of low handicap and professional players, who demand maximum feel and spin for control at all times. This ball is made up of a liquid centre, elastic winding and a Balata cover. It is the cover that gives the feel and control that the expert player is looking for. Balata is a natural substance and is not as durable as some man-made materials used in other types of balls.

A ball being wound.

Many golf balls today have club or company logos put on them. Here the balls are being checked before the logo is stamped on.

THREE-PIECE BALL

The three-piece ball still gives the feel that professionals are looking for, but it has a different cover making it more durable. The centre of the ball is a rubber-type material which is then wound round with rubber thread. The third part of this type of ball is the cover which in many cases is made of surlyn. This is a ball for the serious golfer who is looking for feel and durability.

A two-piece ball.

This shows the make up of the three-piece ball, starting as a pellet which is rounded and then smoothed and wound round with the rubber thread. The cover which is smooth at this stage, is compressed together and the dimple formation pressed on to the cover. The ball is then sprayed and the logo painted on.

TWO-PIECE BALL

The two-piece ball is probably the most popular ball, giving both distance and durability. It is made up of a solid centre and a man-made cover. Because of its hardness this type of ball, whilst travelling further is often difficult to pitch and putt with.

The dimple pattern on the golf ball varies from one make to another; each manufacturer will of course state that theirs is the best! You should try different types and makes of ball finding out which one suits your type of game. The Balata ball is only made in white but the other two types are made in yellow as well.

Balls being painted.

A two-piece ball. The centre of the ball is rounded and then the granules shown here are made into the cover. The cover is a tough material which maintains its shape. The ball is then sprayed and varnished.

OTHER EQUIPMENT

You will find that tee pegs are either wooden or plastic. It is largely a matter of personal preference which type you choose. One of the other items that you will find useful is a ball marker. These small white discs are used to mark the position of the ball on the green if you have to pick it up. A pitch repair fork is handy for repairing indentations made by the ball on the green.

SHOES

The range of golfing shoes on the market today is enormous and can be rather overwhelming. The deciding factor when buying a pair of golf shoes should be comfort as you have to walk a long way in a round of golf. The main choice to be made is whether to buy spiked or non-spiked shoes. Spikes will give you a better grip, but they are heavier and are not really necessary on the lighter parts of the course. If you do wear spikes be careful not to damage the greens.

A pair of spiked golf shoes.

Golf clubs are still made by hand.

PLAYING IN COLD WEATHER

In cold weather it is tempting to wear several layers of clothing to keep warm. However, this will restrict your swing, so it advisable to select lightweight thermal clothing and a waterproof jacket. The majority of waterproof suits are also wind proof. Large mittens are also an excellent way of keeping your hands warm. Select a pair that are lined and easy to take off for each shot. If your hands get cold you will lose control of the club. Always keep your head covered.

If the weather is severe it is probably worth taking fewer clubs as this will speed up play. Keep checking that the studs in your shoes are not clogged, as this can cause you to slip.

PLAYING IN THE RAIN

When playing golf in the rain you will need to wear outer clothing to stay dry. As with the clothing recommended for cold weather, it is important to select a lightweight waterproof jacket that will not restrict your swing. Umbrellas are also useful for protecting yourself and your equipment from the elements between shots.

One of the greatest hazards of playing in the rain is that if the grip becomes sodden it is extremely difficult to keep a firm hold on the club. A clean towel is useful for drying the grip and you can wear all-weather gloves which will enable you to keep a firmer hold. The majority of grips fitted to clubs are made of rubber and you will find that they become less slippery if they are kept clean. The best way to clean them is with a little warm soapy water and a nail brush and then dry them off with a towel. Avoid getting them too wet.

Alternatively many players have their clubs fitted with half or full-cord grips. These grips have cotton thread woven into them which absorbs surface moisture.

It is important to bear in mind that rain gathers on the golf ball which will affect the flight of the ball. Consider using a more lofted club than you would usually, for example, a 5-wood instead of a 3-wood. This will help the ball to become airborne more quickly.

If due to incessant rain your feet sink into the turf at the address your feet will become lower than the level of the ball. To compensate for this move your hands down the grip slightly. If the ground is slippery make sure your shoes are full studded.

Bernhard Langer well wrapped up against the elements in the Dunhill Cup at St Andrews, 1992.

Opposite: Seve Ballesteros

STARTING OUT

One of the things that you hear so often on the golf course is people saying 'Yes, I play golf, but I am so inconsistent'. Golf is a game that is very much in the mind, and you have to work hard at understanding and mastering the basic requirements for consistent and improving play. Everybody wants results, and results come from a sound routine and knowledge of technique, but they also come from confidence.

AIMING THE CLUB

As every shot you play will have a different direction, it is essential to understand how to aim correctly. To ensure that you hit the ball in the right direction you must first be able to imagine the shot you are going to play.

Stand behind your ball to establish the line of flight from the ball to the target – the 'ball-to-target line'. If the target is far away it is easier to start by selecting a point closer to you and in line with the ball and target. Always double-check your aim, and never take it for granted that it is correct.

The part of the club which directs the ball is the leading edge. This must be positioned square to the ball-to-target line and at right angles to your shoulders. This will ensure you have the correct loft on the face of the club.

If the leading edge of the clubface is turned either to the left (a closed face), or out to the right (an open face), this will send the ball off course. Always check the leading edge is square to the ball-to-target line.

THE CLUBHEAD

The toe of the club.

The heel of the club; with an iron this is called the socket.

The face. This is the part of the club with which you usually strike the ball. The ball should be lined up with the centre of the clubface.

POSITION OF THE BALL

The no. 1-wood is correctly positioned to the ball. The ball should be teed-up so that half of the ball is visible above the clubface. Because clubheads have different depths the amount the ball needs to be teed-up will vary.

LIE OF THE CLUB

The lie of this club is too flat, the heel is lifted off the ground.

A

The lie of this club is too upright, the toe is lifted off the ground.

B

This is the correct lie. There should be a slight gap between the toe of the club and the ground.

C

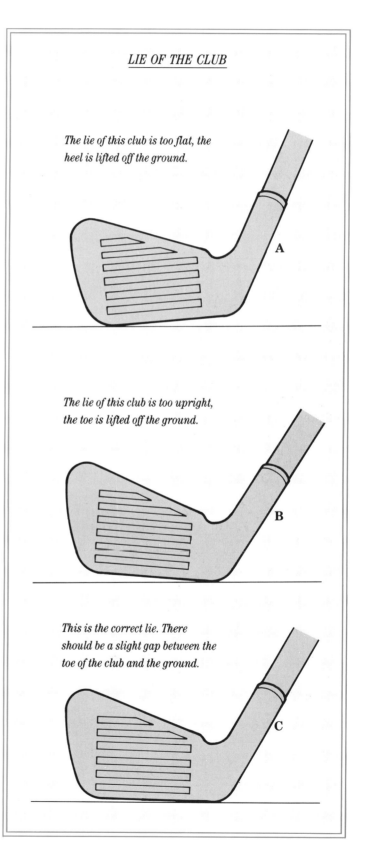

The leading edge. Each clubhead is different in shape and loft but they all have a leading edge. The leading edge must be at right angles to your shoulders and square to the target.

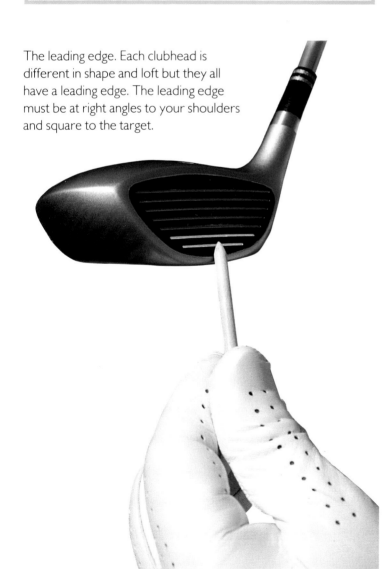

21

OPEN AND CLOSED CLUBFACES

The tees indicate the line to the target
– the 'ball-to-target line'. And here
the 3-wood is set square.

The leading edge is turned to the left,
closing the clubface. This is a frequent
error with this club and should be avoided.

The leading edge is square to the
ball-to-target line.

The toe of the club is turned in,
closing the clubface.

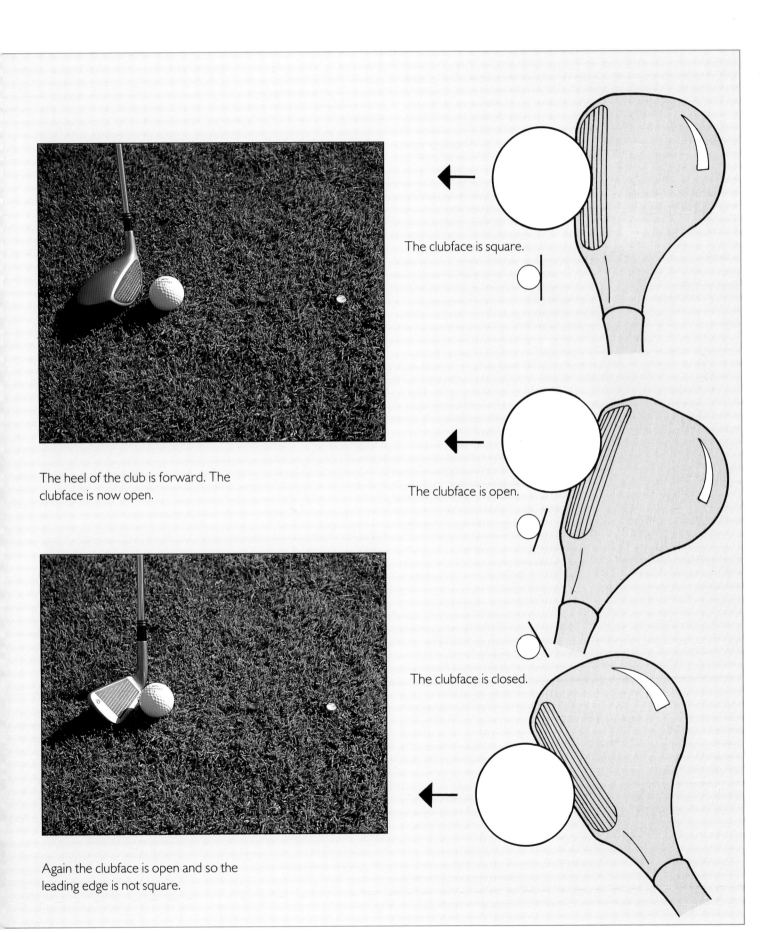

The clubface is square.

The heel of the club is forward. The clubface is now open.

The clubface is open.

The clubface is closed.

Again the clubface is open and so the leading edge is not square.

BALL-TO-TARGET LINE

1 Standing behind the ball will help you to establish the ball-to-target line. This is a good exercise to include in your set-up routine.

2 The clubhead is set on the chosen ball-to-target line.

3 Always double-check your aim by looking at the target.

Key Points Card	
Points	Remarks
1	*Always aim with the leading edge of the golf club.*
2	*Stand behind the ball looking at the target.*
3	*Select a point closer to you on the ball-to-target line.*
4	*Place the clubhead so the ball is in line with the centre of the clubface.*

THE GRIP (HOLD)

There are several different ways of holding the club and you should choose the one that feels most comfortable for you. This will largely depend on the size of your hands. Start by learning the correct hold for the left hand. Do not alter the position of your left hand when you place your right hand on the club. The two hands must be trained to work together, as one unit. The following instructions assume that you are a right-handed player. Reverse the instructions if you are left-handed.

2 The grip of the club should lie diagonally across the palm of your hand approximately ¼ in (6 mm) from the base of your little finger and across to the middle joint of your forefinger.

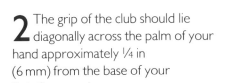

3 When the hand is closed over the grip you should be able to see at least two knuckles on the back of your left hand.

THE LEFT HAND

1 Part of the grip should be outside your left hand. This is more comfortable than holding the end of the grip and will help to give more control.

4 The left thumb needs to be just to the right of the centre of the grip. This will form a V-shape with your forefinger which will point between your face and your right shoulder. To ensure this position is maintained in each shot check that the end of the club and your left hand are in line with the inside of your left leg.

THE RIGHT HAND

1 When you place your right hand on the grip make sure you do not move the position of your left hand. The palm of the right hand faces the target. The grip should lie in the middle joints of the first three fingers.

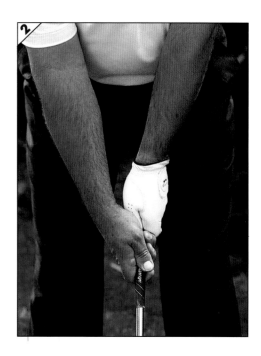

2 The left thumb will now fit inside the right hand as you close your hand over the grip. The right thumb should lie just to the left of the centre of the grip. It should also form a V-shape.

3 Both 'V's must point between your face and right shoulder.

TYPES OF GRIP (HOLD)

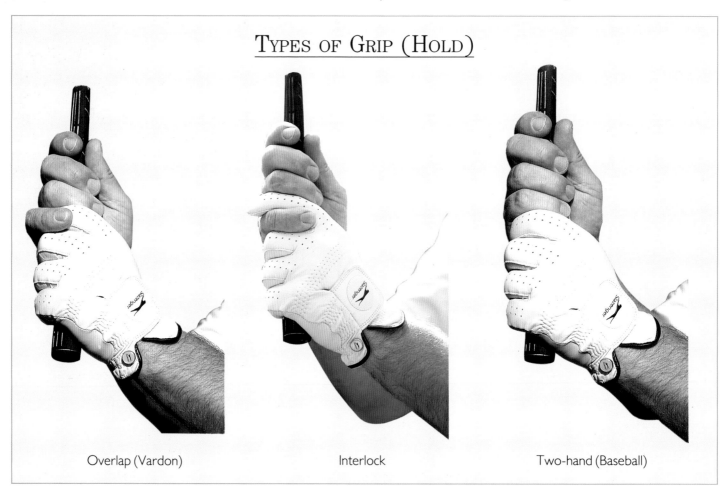

| Overlap (Vardon) | Interlock | Two-hand (Baseball) |

THE PROFESSIONALS

Harry Vardon, c. 1905. The overlapping grip is otherwise known as the Vardon grip because Vardon was considered to be one of the first great players to use this type of hold on the club. This is the most popular of the three grips.

GRIP PRESSURE

1 It is important to maintain the correct pressure on the grip. To control the club at the top of the backswing you need to feel you are holding the club with the last three fingers of your left hand. This gives you control and at the same time enables wrist movement. In your right hand feel the pressure in your middle two fingers.

2 The hands should always be close together to enable them to work as a single unit.

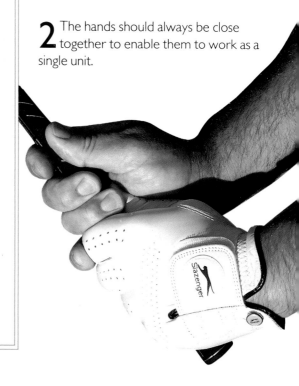

3 Your hold on the club should be maintained throughout the swing.

4 The face of the club is in the correct position at the top of the backswing. The palms of the hands and the clubface are working together.

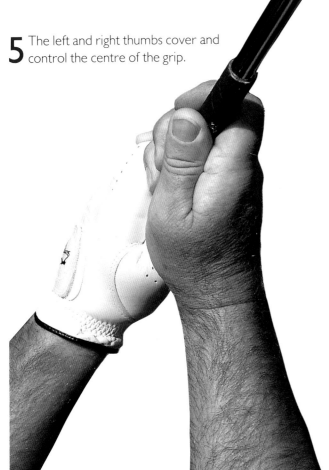

5 The left and right thumbs cover and control the centre of the grip.

GRIPS FOR WOMEN AND YOUNGER PLAYERS

The two-handed and interlocking holds are often used by women and younger golfers as they are more suited to players with smaller hands. This picture shows a sound two-handed grip.

THE PROFESSIONALS

Arnold Palmer of the USA using the overlapping hold on the club. See how his hands are held high. This was a feature of the great man's play in his heyday. His hands have kept complete control of the club.

COMMON FAULTS

You will often find that if you are having problems with your swing these have occurred because you have the wrong grip. Watch out for the faults shown below and always check you have the right grip.

Key Points Card

Points	Remarks
1	*Once you have the correct left-hand grip, do not alter it when you place your right hand on the club.*
2	*Remember the position of the thumbs helps to control the position of the clubface at the top of the backswing.*
3	*Maintain the correct grip pressure. You must not let go of the club during the shot.*

STRONG GRIP

1 The 'V's formed by the forefingers and thumbs are pointing to the right of the right shoulder. This tends to take loft off the clubface and causes the clubhead to become shut.

2 See how the face of the club is pointing to the sky, which can result in hooking the ball left, hitting the ball low left or fluffing (hitting the ground before impact with the ball).

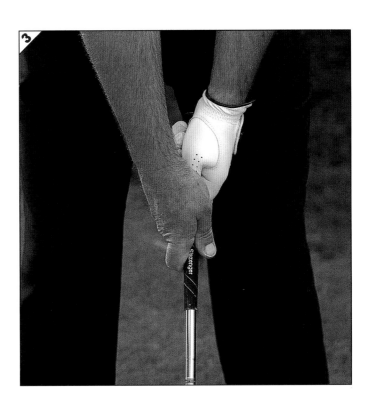

WEAK GRIP

3 & 4 Here the hands are pointing towards the left shoulder. This will increase the loft on the clubface during the backswing and lead to the clubface looking down to the ground. The ball will probably be sliced to the right.

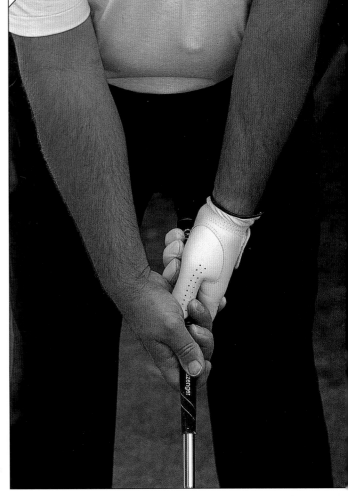

5 The left thumb is extended down the grip of the club. The danger is that it will be difficult to place the right hand correctly on the club, causing a loss of hand control.

STANCE

Having established how to hold and aim the club it is now important to check your posture. Without the correct posture you will find it extremely hard to keep good balance and create the correct movements. Follow the steps shown and in particular note the angle of the spine.

It is largely a matter of personal preference as to how far your feet are apart. This distance will also vary depending on the club you are playing with. But as a general rule your feet should be shoulder width apart when playing with woods and then moved closer together for shorter clubs.

1 Relax. Stand with your arms at your sides and feet shoulder width apart.

2 Bend forward from the hips. Your hips should go back and your head and shoulders forward. Keep your back straight.

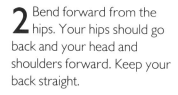

3 Maintaining the same spinal angle, let your arms hang down freely from your shoulders.

BODY ALIGNMENT

1 This now leads us on to body alignment. Shoulders, hips, knees and feet should be square, parallel to the ball.

BODY ALIGNMENT

To obtain the correct alignment to the target imagine a railway line – the clubhead, ball and target are on one rail and your feet, knees, hips and shoulders on the other. This will help you ensure that the clubhead and ball are set square and that you are standing parallel to the target. This is called a square set-up.

2 Holding the club, flex your legs slightly, and let your hands hang down comfortably. Your right forearm will be slightly lower than your left arm. Head neither up nor down.

POSTURE

To help yourself adopt the correct posture follow the routine shown below for every shot you play.

1 First stand upright, check that you have a square set-up – parallel to the ball-to-target line.

2 Keeping your back straight lean forward and flex your legs towards one another.

POSTURE FROM BEHIND

3 Notice how the spine tilts to the right. This should occur naturally if the shoulders are square, with the left hand at the top of the grip.

4 Note how the feet are wider apart now that a longer club is being used.

BALL POSITION

The position of the ball in relation to your feet will vary according to the length of the club. With longer clubs the ball is further forward in the stance (just inside the left heel). As the club gets shorter move the ball back towards the middle of the stance. The ball is also positioned further away from the player when longer clubs are used.

1 The body is square to the ball-to-target line.

MEDIUM SHOTS

3 For the medium clubs note how the ball has moved further back in the stance. Its position is more central.

LONG SHOTS

2 Position the ball so it forms a right angle from just inside your left foot to the ball-to-target line. Feet shoulder width apart.

4 As the club gets shorter move your feet closer together. Head still behind the ball.

SUMMARY

In each of the following three pictures the same grip – the overlap – is being used for each type of club. In each case the club is extended from the left arm and the left hand is in line with the inside of the left leg. You can see clearly that both 'V's are pointing between the face and right shoulder. If you looked down the club from this position you would be able to see two or three knuckles on the back of the left hand.

As the club gets shorter then the ball is positioned further back in the stance and the feet move closer together.

LONG SHOTS

1 Ball inside the left foot, feet shoulder width apart, head behind the ball and weight evenly distributed.

MEDIUM SHOTS

2 Ball central in the stance, feet slightly closer together and arms hanging down comfortably.

EXERCISE

This exercise without a club shows the correct hand, arm and body movements for the takeaway. You need the correct posture to do this. Follow through to a point about waist high. From this small movement you can learn the correct co-ordination needed for consistent and improving play.

SHORT SHOTS

3 Ball further back in the stance and closer to the player, and slightly more weight on the left leg.

ey Points Card

nts	Remarks
1	*Without the correct posture you will find it extremely hard to remain well-balanced and to swing correctly.*
2	*Timing, rhythm and balance are the key to a good swing.*
3	*Aim, grip, posture, body alignment and ball position have to be correct and consistent to enable you to improve.*

THE PROFESSIONALS

Severiano Ballesteros of Spain is seen here checking his aim before driving. He is using the overlapping (Vardon) grip. His arms are hanging down comfortably from a good posture.

THE SWING

Having mastered the routine for making a good sound address position you are ready to attempt the movements required for the best possible golf swing. The following four series of pictures show the movements for the long (full), medium and short swing. Following this, the separate elements of the swing – grip and ball alignment, the takeaway, the backswing, the downswing and the swing path – are examined in more detail. Remember to check your aim, grip and stance before you start the swing.

THE PROFESSIONALS

Nancy Lopez of the USA playing in England in 1978. This picture shows the complete follow-through which is a feature of a good swing.

THE FULL SWING

1 Position the ball level with the inside of the left foot. Stand with a relaxed posture and alignment.

4 Transfer body-weight on to your left side. Release the clubhead to the target with your arms together.

2 The takeaway should be a single movement, with your wrists not cocking before waist height.

3 At the top of the backswing, make a full shoulder turn. The club shaft should be parallel to the target line.

5 Bend your right leg at the knee. Turn your shoulders through, allowing your head to look at the result.

6 At this point your hands should be high and your arms together and well-balanced. Maintain the grip.

THE MEDIUM SWING

1 Position the ball centrally in your stance and stand with your arms hanging down comfortably.

2 Your arms and body should move together but do not cock your wrists until waist height.

3 Keep your head steady and do not take the club as far back in the medium swing as in the full swing.

THE SHORT SWING

1 Note the position of the arms and wrists. You cock your wrists much earlier for the short swing.

2 Take the club up much more quickly, with less left foot and body movement.

3 Don't take your hands much higher than your shoulders. Note the hand and wrist position.

4 As you start the downswing, your legs and arms should work together. Transfer weight on to your left leg.

5 Your head is brought through the swing by your right shoulder.

6 The movement in body-weight should take the left shoe over slightly.

4 Keep your wrists cocked as you start the downswing.

5 Head steady at impact.

6 Balanced follow-through, with your arms together.

WOMEN'S SWING

Even though women have a different physique from men, the same principles of the golf swing apply. They have to control the clubhead and the direction of the down and through swing. However, a good posture is particularly essential to enable the female player to make a good shoulder turn, both on the backswing and follow-through, as well as a good free arm movement.

3 Fold your right arm with your elbow pointing down to the ground, the shaft of the club should be parallel to the ball-to-target line.

2 This picture shows a good one-piece takeaway, with the hands and the clubhead working together.

1 Stand with a good posture, your arms hanging down, body aligned square and legs flexed at the knee.

4 After impact your hands are at waist height, your head should be steady and left arm about to fold.

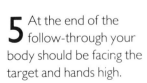

5 At the end of the follow-through your body should be facing the target and hands high.

THE PROFESSIONALS

Dottie Mochrie of America is seen here clearing the lower half of the body through impact so that the arms and club can be swung towards the target.

43

GRIP AND BALL ALIGNMENT

The address position is a rehearsal for the impact the clubhead is going to make with the ball. As your hands are your only physical contact with the club their position in relation to the golf ball is very important.

HANDS TOO FAR BACK

1 Both hands and the grip of the club are behind the ball. Looking down the club at the ball both hands will be to the right of the ball. This could cause the hand action on the takeaway to be too late.

HANDS TOO FAR FORWARD

2 Both hands and the grip of the club are in front of the ball. Looking down the club both hands will be to the left of the ball. This position could cause an early wrist cock.

CORRECT POSITION

3 The left hand just covers the inside of the left leg and is in line with the left side of the ball. The palm of the right hand and the leading edge of the golf club are aligned with the back of the ball. This is where the hands and club should be at impact.

RIGHT HAND

1 The palm of the hand should be in line with the back of the ball and facing the ball-to-target line.

2 This shows the position of the hand relative to the ball when holding the grip of the club.

LEFT HAND

3 The back of the left hand should be facing the target and hanging over the left side of the ball.

THE GRIP

5 The hands are in the overlap grip. Both palms are facing one another, and both 'V's are pointing in the same direction.

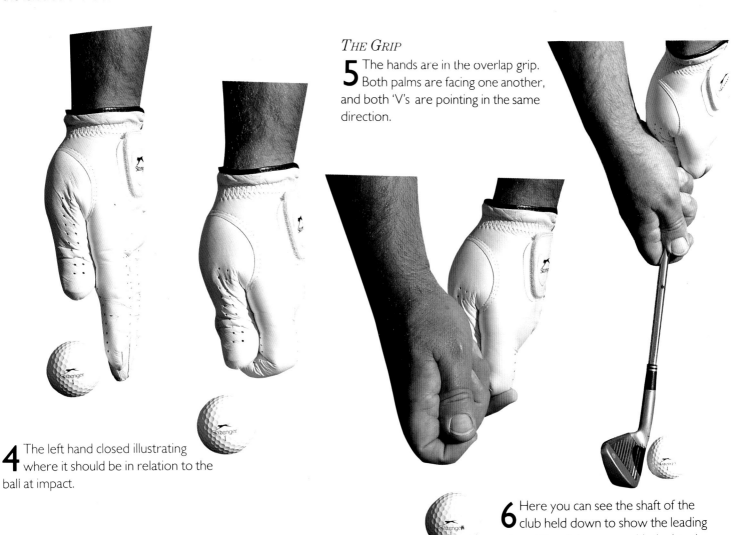

4 The left hand closed illustrating where it should be in relation to the ball at impact.

6 Here you can see the shaft of the club held down to show the leading edge of the club square with the hands.

TAKEAWAY AND BACKSWING

The takeaway is the beginning of the backswing. This must be a one-piece movement, with the left and right sides moving together. Throughout this part of the swing your elbows must remain the same distance apart as they were at the address, and you must keep the head of the club square with your shoulders.

Note the difference in angle that occurs between long and short clubs.

No. 1-WOOD

1 From the address position, the club, arms, shoulders, hips and legs move as one unit. As the club and arms travel beyond the right side body-weight is transferred on to the instep of the right foot. This should not be a conscious action and must happen smoothly and naturally. The left hand, the back of which was pointing towards the target, will now face away from you.

2 From behind the ball you can see how the arms move together and have stayed the same distance apart as they were at the address. The clubhead, shaft and grip are an extension of the left arm. This unit is parallel with the ball-to-target line.

3 This shows the completed backswing for all long clubs. The shoulders have turned 90° and the hips 45°. The angle of the spine is the same as it was at the address. The hands have kept total contact with the golf club and maintained a square clubface. The left arm is comfortably straight and the right arm bent with the elbow pointing to the ground just behind the right foot.

SHORT IRON

1 The wrists cock sooner at the start of the backswing with the short iron. The hands and arms are used to make the action, rather than the body, enabling you to maintain the angle set at the address.

2 Again the left arm and the club on the ground are in line with one another. Because the ball is now closer to you the club will come up at a steeper angle. This in turn will give a steeper attack on the ball. Short iron clubheads are more rounded so when the ball is struck it runs up the face of the club causing backspin.

3 At the top of the swing the wrists are fully cocked at shoulder height. The head is steady and there is less body movement than with longer clubs.

4 From a different angle you can see how there is less body movement. The hands are controlling the clubface, the arms are together and swinging freely from the chest.

LONG AND SHORT CLUBS

1 With the long clubs, the arms and club move without an early wrist action, whereas with shorter clubs the wrists take the club back.

2 Note how the angle you swing the club away from the ball alters with the distance that you stand from the ball.

Key Points Card

Points	Remarks
1	*Make sure the takeaway is a one-piece movement.*
2	*Ensure your body-weight is transferred smoothly on to the instep of your right foot.*
3	*Keep the clubhead square to your shoulders.*
4	*Keep your left arm straight and avoid an early wrist cock when using long clubs.*
5	*Keep your head still, looking at the ball.*

THE PROFESSIONALS

Curtis Strange of America is seen here just after impact. His head is held steady and his right leg and foot are transferring weight on to the left side.

THE PROFESSIONALS

Greg Norman of Australia is one of the world's most exciting players. This picture shows the force with which he hits the ball, allowing the right shoulder and right side to keep moving through impact and his very individual foot action.

EXERCISE

Practise holding the shaft of the club further down. This will help keep the whole of the club as part of your left arm and work on the shoulder hip and leg movement at the start of the swing. See how when you cock the wrists the handle of the club breaks away from your arm.

THE DOWNSWING AND FOLLOW-THROUGH

The downswing starts from the moment you complete the takeaway of the club and describes the path of the clubhead from the top of the backswing down to the ball on impact. The follow-through describes the path of the club after impact. The club, wrists, arms, body and legs must all work smoothly together so that the clubhead arrives square-on to the ball.

LONG CLUBS

1 The lower part of the body moves towards the target as the arms come down from the top of the backswing with the wrists still cocked. This keeps the head steady and the right shoulder back at the start of the downswing, ensuring the shoulders will be square to the ball-to-target line at impact.

2 The whole of the right side continues to move through impact unrestricted by the head. Note the width of the arc the club has made at this point.

3 Hands high, body well-balanced and spinal angle maintained. This shot will finish just to the left of the centre of the fairway in pole position.

MEDIUM CLUBS

1 With medium length clubs the legs and arms again pull the club down, with the head held steady.

2 The arms and shoulders swing the club through to the target moving underneath the head.

Key Points Card

Points	Remarks
1	_From the top of the backswing the club, wrists, arms, body and legs must all work together._
2	_Transfer your weight smoothly from right to left._
3	_Hit through the ball, keeping your head down and a still body position._
4	_Follow through until your hips and body are facing the target._

3 The body is facing the target with body-weight on the left side. See how the divot was taken after impact.

SHORT IRONS

1 With the short iron it is a downward strike. Again, the shoulders are back ready to be square to the target at impact.

2 This is an unrestricted movement through the shot with the left side.

3 The water was no problem because the club had plenty of loft and did not stop on the shot.

LONG SHOT

The downswing has brought the weight of the body on to the left side; the shoulders are square to the target, and the legs clear the hips to allow the hands and arms to extend and swing the clubhead to the target. With both male and female golfers a good posture at the address is essential to keep the upper half of the body square to the ball-to-target line at impact. Here we see the spinal angle is being maintained to enable the right shoulder to be lower through impact than the left shoulder.

THE PROFESSIONALS

Fred Couples of the USA is one of the best players in the world. He is seen here showing a well-balanced follow-through. The angle of the spine is maintained throughout the shot.

SHORT SHOT

The downswing movements through the legs and hips transfer weight on to the left side and keep the club low to the ground at, and after, impact. The hands, arms and clubhead have moved together through impact.

Swing Path

In the first picture (1) the ground between the player and the golf club is called 'the inside', and the ground on the other side is called 'the outside'. The correct swing path is from 'in-to-square', and 'in' again. This means that the clubhead is taken back on the inside, and after impact the follow-through should continue on the inside.

I The ground between the player and the golf clubs on the ball-to-target line is called 'the inside'.

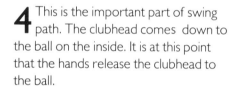

2 On the takeaway, due to the body pivoting the club travels over the ground called the inside.

3 And onwards to the top of the backswing. This shows a good angle to the backswing.

4 This is the important part of swing path. The clubhead comes down to the ball on the inside. It is at this point that the hands release the clubhead to the ball.

5 Through impact, the clubhead is square and the hips are out of the way helping to keep the shoulders square to the ball-to-target line.

6 After impact the body continues to move through to face the target causing the club to swing on the inside.

7 A good extension of the arms takes the club past waist height. The arms are together and body-weight is on the outside of the left shoe.

8 Complete follow-through. The body has moved to face the target and watch the result.

SWING PATH

The direction the clubhead is travelling in at impact will govern how the ball will start in its flight. In-to-out and the ball will start right of the target. Out-to-in and the ball will start left of the target. In-to-square and in again and the ball will fly straight.

In-to-out

Out-to-in

Ball-to-target line

SWING PATH: EXAMPLE TWO

1 & 2 These two pictures show the club moving towards the target. The head is held steady, shoulders square, weight on the left leg, and right foot moving on to the instep, with the leg bending at the knee helping the hips to clear.

FLIGHT PATH

If the ball swerves in its flight it is because it has side spin on it. This is caused by the position of the clubface at impact, and the swing path. The clubface should be square at impact. Hit with an open face the ball will swerve to the right and with a closed face to the left.

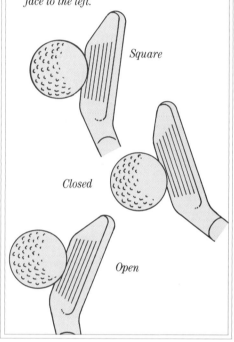

Square

Closed

Open

3 & 4 The clubhead is square to the shoulders with the toe of the club having overtaken the heel and beginning to point to the sky. Note the position of the right arm and how the left forearm and elbow are helping to keep the arms together. The head is still.

5 & 6 Body facing the target, hands under the club, right shoe up on to the toe and right shoulder still slightly lower than the left. The hold on the grip of the club is the same as it was at the address.

SWING PATH: EXAMPLE THREE

1 Address all set. Shoulders square. See how the arms are hanging down and the back is straight and tilted over the ground. Head clear of chest.

2 Moving down on the inside this is a good swing path. Hips clearing and shoulders ready to move squarely through impact.

3 Notice the divot is square with the line-up and that the club is now travelling over the inside.

4 The follow-through is complete. The angle of spine is the same as for the address. The divot has gone to the left of the target, indicating the clubhead moved from square to the inside, through impact.

WARM-UP EXERCISES

ARMS AND HANDS

It is essential in the playing of all golf shots that you maintain your hold on the grip of the club. To enable you to do this from the start warm up before you play. This exercise will give you a stretching feeling in your arms and also rehearse the action of the arms for the backswing. Repeat this exercise several times. Then repeat the movement in the same way but taking the club to your left side. While you are doing this feel the pressure of your hold on the club in the last three fingers of your left hand and practise maintaining it throughout the action.

1 Stand in the address position.

2 Standing upright, lift the club up above your head and between your right shoulder and the right side of your head. Keep your arms the same distance apart at the elbows as they were in the address position.

3 Repeat this action for the left side, lifting the club up between your left shoulder and left side of your head.

SHOULDERS

These movements are designed to help you
understand and practise the correct shoulder
movements and angle of the spine.

1 Hold the golf club in front of you,
across your chest. Assume the
correct posture.

2 Keeping your head still, turn your
shoulders so that the grip points
outside your right shoe. The hips and legs
also respond to this shoulder turn. It is
important to train yourself to turn
around the spine position set at the
address, for it is the spine that gives the
tilt to the shoulder turn.

3 From the backswing
position, keeping your
head still, transfer your weight
with a leg and hip movement.
Bring your shoulders down and
around to complete a follow-through
position. Notice that the head of the club
is now well past the left shoe showing
the shoulder turn on the follow-through
is greater than that on the backswing.
Note how this shoulder movement turns
your head so that it is looking along
the ball-to-target line.

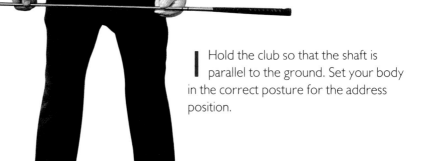

HIPS

Both the shoulder and hip actions are essential to give the arms and hands the correct angle of attack on the golf ball. Repeat these hip movements several times. The main point to note here is that the hips turn on a line parallel to the ground.

I Hold the club so that the shaft is parallel to the ground. Set your body in the correct posture for the address position.

2 Keeping your head still, turn your body with the golf club parallel to the ground. This practises the correct hip turn on the backswing.

3 Here you can see the hip and leg action on the follow-through. During this action you should turn your hips rather than tilting them.

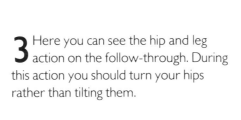

THE SWING

The golf swing is a series of movements, not least of all of the golf club itself. Although people say let the club do the work in fact the club can do very little on its own, and this final exercise will help you accelerate the movement of the club.

For many right-handed golfers it may take some time and effort, to train the left arm and hand to make these movements, as it will for left-handed golfers with the right arm, but in time you will be able to achieve these positions. Being able to understand and perform them is of great importance if you are to play golf to your full potential.

1 Hold any club quite far down the grip and roughly in the centre of the stance but with your right hand only.

2 Take the club back a short distance, note how the right arm bends at the elbow.

3 Now swing the club with your hand and arm across your shoulder line as fast as you can. Maintain your hold on the grip of the club. This should give you the feeling of releasing the clubhead past your body. Repeat this action several times. The reason for holding the grip of the club in the middle is that it ensures you do not hit the ground.

5 Swing the club back a short distance with your left arm and hand, and then accelerate the club across your shoulder line as fast as you can while maintaining your hold on the grip. Again you do not want to hit the ground. Notice how the left arm bends at the elbow and also the shape of the clubhead at this point.

4 Next hold the grip of the club with your left hand. Position the club in the centre of your stance.

EXERCISE

This exercise is an aid to showing you, through sound, at which point you should be making the club accelerate. Take any club; hold it the wrong way around. Make a full back and through swing as if hitting a ball. The shaft and grip will make a swishing sound as the club is swung down and through. The noise should occur at and after the area of impact.

6 Again this should give you the feeling of releasing the clubhead and shaft past your body.

STRETCHING

1 Taking two or three clubs with similar lengths of shafts, set up for the address position. Do not use a ball. Because you are using more than one club you will not be able to create a correct hold on the club, but make sure that you can control how far the clubs go back on the backswing and the follow-through.

2 & 3 Make this full swing as shown here, avoid hitting the ground as you swing through. The weight of the clubs will help you in stretching the arm and shoulder movement.

Opposite: Ian Woosnam

THE SHORT GAME

Having learnt the basics of the game of golf, it
is important to adapt these skills so that you
can play shots from different parts of the
course. Greenside shots may require either a
short high ball, the pitch, or a low, running ball,
the chip. The pitch requires a lofted club to lift
up the ball over a hazard, while the chip
requires a straighter-faced club so that the ball
flies away on a lower trajectory.

PITCHING

The pitch is used when you need the ball to fly high in the air over a hazard, such as a bunker or a bank. A lofted club – the sand or pitching wedge – is used to give the ball lift. Your choice of club will depend on the lie of the ball and the distance to the target. The pitching wedge is the more versatile of these two clubs because the sand wedge must only be used in a bunker or on a soft, grassy lie. You can also vary the strength of the pitch by how far down the grip you hold the club.

The pitch is what is called a 'pressure' shot because it is a chance for you to improve your score. If you fail to send the ball high it may also end up in a bunker!

2 Here you can see the distance from the ball to the target. With the bunkers in the way the ball must go in the air.

3 Use the full length of the club for this shot. Check the club and ball are lined up to the target, the flag. Nothing is in the way of the swing path – the shoulders are square with the feet, legs and hips open.

1 Set the leading edge square. Position the ball slightly off centre, closer to the heel of the club. Stand with the left foot back to give an open stance.

4 Turn your shoulders and legs slightly for the swing but the main action is in your hands and arms. Keep your head quite still and make sure your hands and the clubface are in shape together.

5 This shot was a ball-and-turf contact, caused by the shift in body-weight and the hands and arms hitting down and through at impact.

7 Move on to the instep of your right foot, helping your hips through. The loft of the club is still in view.

6 At impact shift your weight on to the left side, clearing the hips. With your shoulders still square, your arms and golf club send the ball to the flag.

8 Watch the result with the club pointing directly at the flag.

THE SHORT PITCH

1 If the ball is lying in nice soft grass use the sand wedge. Maintain the same grip as before but position the ball slightly further back in the stance. This picture gives the impression that the hands are ahead of the ball but in fact the left hand is still in line with the inside of the left leg. Put more weight on the left leg and stand with feet, hips and legs slightly open.

2 Take the club back with an early wrist cock, supporting the movement with your shoulders. There should be very little movement of your left leg and hips. The whole of the face of the club is visible.

3 At impact your left arm, the shaft and head of the club return in to line, as they were at the address position. Transfer your body-weight over to the left side, to help keep the clubhead low through the shot. It is essential to keep your head still and shoulders square.

4 The right side should move under your head and shoulders allowing your arms to swing the club to the target. The arms and the whole of the club work together. It is the shape of the clubhead that gives the ball height and direction.

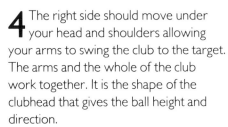

PITCHING

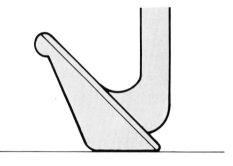

This is how the sole of the pitching wedge sits on the ground.

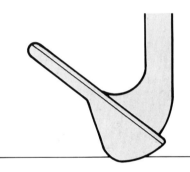

The leading edge of the sand wedge is off the ground. The back of the sole is rounded to give the bounce you need to move enough sand to get the ball out of the greenside bunker.

When attempting a pitch shot it is very important to remember that it is the loft on the clubface that lifts the ball into the air. It is not a lifting action made by the body and hands.

In the first picture the leading edge is square to the ball, presenting the correct loft on the clubface. On the takeaway and backswing the body stays still as the wrists and arms take the club back and up.

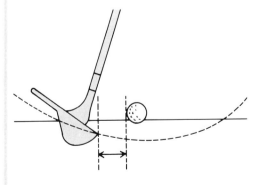

The distance between the ball and the club should be between 1½ and 2 ins (35–50 mm)

A SHORT HIGH LOB SHOT

1 When addressing the ball for a short, high, lob shot to a raised green your legs should be more flexed at the knee. Position the ball quite close to your feet and not too far back in the stance.

2 Just before impact keep your wrists cocked and pull the club down to the ball with your arms and body-weight.

3 Keeping your head steady, but in no way forced down, make a smooth transference of weight on to your left side with your feet, legs and hips. The clubhead should still be extended from the shoulders.

4 Follow through with your right shoulder lower than your left. Your head should naturally turn to face the target. Notice that the loft can still be seen on the face of the club.

5 Watch the result from a well-balanced position.

THE PITCHING WEDGE

The pitching wedge is a very versatile golf club which is used to play high shots to the green from many different distances.

In the series of pictures on the following page note that the distance of the ball from the feet slightly increases as the length of the shot increases, and the arms and shoulders swing the club back further as the shot being played gets longer.

In each case the hands and arms are working together to create a square impact. The head is held steady and the weight of the lower body moves on to the left side, with shoulders becoming square to the ball at impact. The angle of the spine is maintained through impact and as the shot being played gets longer the clubhead is released in a slightly different way. The extent that the body moves through the shot increases with the longer pitching wedge shots.

To learn just what you can achieve with the pitching wedge you need to spend time playing shots of varying distances. Find out how much arm-swing and body movement you personally have to make to hit the ball different distances. Always watch the results. You must learn to play all these shots from memory which will require a sound technique and plenty of practice.

Striking with the pitching or sand wedge is what is called a ball-turf-contact. This is achieved with the correct movements of the lower body-weight, and the arms and club on the downswing and through impact. It is very important that you do not let the club overtake your arms as you hit the ball. You must never try and lift the ball off the ground up into the air, use the loft on the clubface.

This series of pictures illustrate the changes that occur in the swing as the player moves further back from the target. In each case the club is swung further back as the shot being played gets longer.

PITCHING WEDGE SHOTS FROM DIFFERENT DISTANCES

In each of the four series of pictures the player is further away from the target. Notice how the distance that the club is swung back and the extent the body moves through the shot increase with the longer shots.

THE PROFESSIONALS

Nick Faldo of England playing a pitch up and over a bank to the green.
The clubface has still got loft on it. Notice how he is not wearing a glove
on his left hand. Many of the best players remove their glove for pitching,
chipping and putting.

CHIPPING

This is a shot played from various distances from the putting surface when you need a low running ball, rather than a high ball. You can use your putter for this shot but often the fairway or the approach to the green is too wet, or not smooth enough, to roll the ball over. The ideal club loft for this shot is a 4-iron, but as the shot is played with the ball positioned quite close to your feet and the 4-iron shaft is quite long it might get caught up in your clothing. To avoid this occurring use a 6- or a 7-iron.

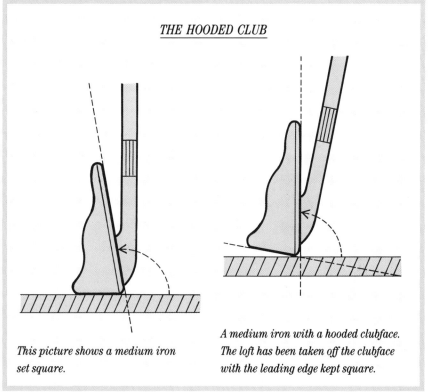

THE HOODED CLUB

This picture shows a medium iron set square.

A medium iron with a hooded clubface. The loft has been taken off the clubface with the leading edge kept square.

1 When you set the leading edge square your hands should be a little ahead of the ball, this has the effect of taking loft from the face of the club, so that it is not closed but hooded. Position the ball slightly back in the stance and stand with your body-weight a little more on the left leg than on the right. Notice how close the ball is to the feet.

2 Move your arms, hands and club back together with no wrist break, keeping the clubhead low to the ground. The clubface should still be hooded.

3 Just before impact the clubhead and shaft, and hands and arms, should return to the same position as in the address. Keep your body very still.

4 As you follow through your wrists should not move and you should keep the body quite still. The ball will fly away low to the ground.

5 Move your arms and club towards the target as one unit. Take them forward at least as far as they went back on the backswing. During this action keep your legs still and shoulders square.

6 Watch the result.

CLOSE TO THE
PUTTING SURFACE

1 Look at the spot where you would like the ball to land and then run up to and in the hole.

2 Set the ball quite close to your feet and hold the grip of the club quite low down. Body-weight just slightly more on your left side which will help keep the clubhead low through impact.

3 The action is a movement of the hands and arms, not the body. The clubhead should still be hooded and low to the ground.

4 Swing your arms and club together so that impact is slow and smooth. Keep your body still and shoulders square to the ball-to-target line.

5 The clubhead should remain low to the ground as it moves towards the target. Do not cock your wrists. Keep your body and head still.

6 Follow through at least as far forward as you went back on the backswing. The ball is running towards the target.

1 Hold the grip of the club slightly further up than for the other chipping shots to help make a longer backswing. Feet, legs and hips open.

CHIPPING FROM FURTHER AWAY

2 Cock your wrists in order to swing the club further back and hit the ball a greater distance. Little to no body movement.

3 Bring the clubhead into the ball low to the ground. Note the movement of the right leg.

4 Your club, hands and arms should be working smoothly together with your right leg and side moving towards the target. Some grass will be moved at impact.

5 Watch the result with the clubhead and the ball still in line with one another. The ball is low and ready to run.

Key Points Card

Points	Remarks
1	*Always use the correct hold on the club.*
2	*Select the correct club and decide where you want the ball to land on the green.*
3	*Keep the body still during the shot.*
4	*Use little to no wrist action.*
5	*Keep the clubhead low to the ground.*
6	*Swing the club backwards and forwards the same distance.*

THE CHIP SHOT

The chip is a low running shot, therefore you need to take loft off the clubface. Select a club that has a comfortable length of shaft. At the address set your hands slightly ahead of the ball, this will deloft the club. The clubface is now hooded.

On the takeaway, there is no wrist break, the clubhead is still hooded, the body stays steady and the clubhead is low to the ground.

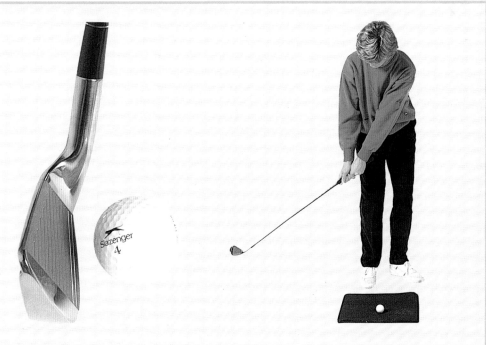

PUTTING

Putts are probably the most pressurized shots on the golf course. In no area is practise more important. Practise so that you feel confident with your putting action, able to judge distances and able to read the green. The importance of putting is illustrated by the old golfing phrase, 'You drives for show, but you putts for dough'.

PUTTING

Putting is an area of the game that is neglected by many club and higher handicap players. This may be because the green is an accessible part of the golf course and if you fail to putt the ball then 'all the world' can see. Very few people are prepared to spend time on the practice green and practise is what is usually required.

Concentration and confidence play a big role in all golf shots, and at no time are they more important than when putting. You only have to watch how much time and care the professional players put into the preparation of their shots on the putting green to see how much concentration is required. Confidence will come from good sound technique and practice. Always remember that however close you are to the hole, do not trust to luck. Take care to line up for the shot. Putting is never as easy as it looks.

I The putter head is set square to the target with the ball in the centre of the clubface. A reverse overlap grip is being used and the arms are extended down. Ball positioned just left of centre in the stance, the body is evenly balanced. Head positioned over the ball.

2 At the takeaway the head and body are kept still as the club is taken back with a movement of the arms and shoulders. Try and avoid using wrist action when putting. Move the whole of the putter – the head, shaft and grip – with a pendular movement of the arms.

3 On the follow-through the head and body are kept still, and the whole club swung with the arms, using no wrist break. How far the putter is taken back and through will depend on the length of the putt and the speed of the green.

Opposite: Jack Nicklaus.

BALL ALIGNMENT

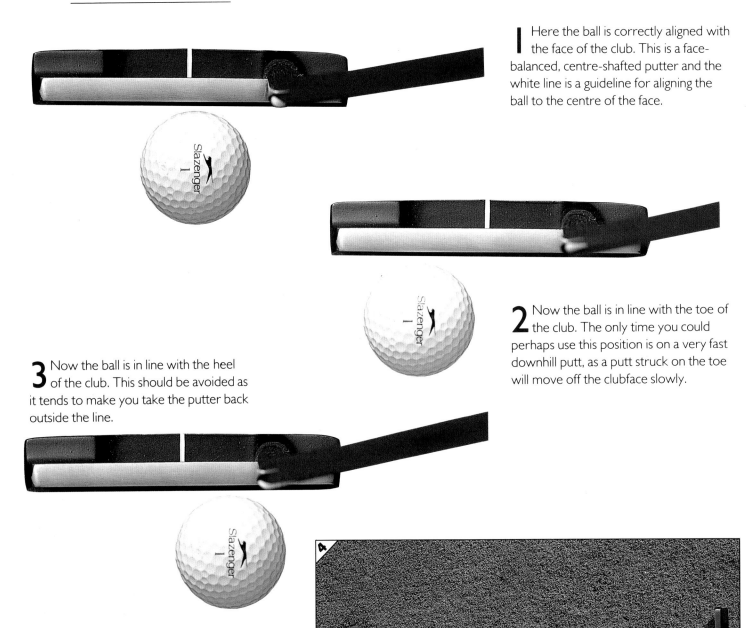

I Here the ball is correctly aligned with the face of the club. This is a face-balanced, centre-shafted putter and the white line is a guideline for aligning the ball to the centre of the face.

2 Now the ball is in line with the toe of the club. The only time you could perhaps use this position is on a very fast downhill putt, as a putt struck on the toe will move off the clubface slowly.

3 Now the ball is in line with the heel of the club. This should be avoided as it tends to make you take the putter back outside the line.

4 This line of balls indicates how you should imagine the ball moving off the face of the putter and rolling in to the hole. As in all shots aiming is very important.

THE GRIP

1 Put both hands close together, with thumbs on the top of the grip and the index finger of your left hand outside the middle three fingers of your right hand. The index finger of the right hand should go down the grip.

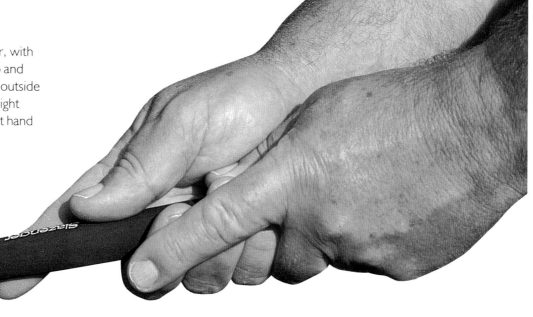

2 A different view of the hands. This is called the reverse overlap grip and it is just one of many ways you can hold the putter. Whichever way you hold the putter you must make sure it becomes part of your arms because a good pulling action avoids independent wrist movement. The pressure of the grip should be quite soft so that you feel you are moving the head with your arms and shoulders.

3 Holding the head over the hole like this shows that the face of the club is square to the target, the hole.

THE PROFESSIONALS

Bernhard Langer of Germany showing his very individual way of holding the club when putting.

BALL-TO-TARGET LINE

View from behind the line of the putt. The line of the feet and body is square with the ball-to-target line.

THE ADDRESS

It is important to keep the body out of the way to enable free movement of the putter back and through. The ball is in line with the inside of the left shoe which will help to create top spin and make the ball roll. Your head should be directly over the ball and hands held away and out from the legs. This helps to cut down the use of the wrists. Body-weight well-balanced as you will be standing still throughout the stroke.

THE SHORT PUTT

The putt shown here is a good length to practise with. Given that putting is largely a question of confidence it is often better to practise with putts that you are likely to hole rather than destroying your confidence by missing longer ones.

I Hold the grip and check that the 'V' of your left hand is pointing to your left shoulder and that the 'V' of your right hand is pointing to your right shoulder. This will help keep your arms and hands together as one unit. Remember that for the putt the address position is well-balanced and that the ball lines up with the inside of your left shoe.

2 In the short putt take the putter low to the ground as one unit from your shoulders. The distance that the putter goes back will depend on the length of the shot and the speed of the green.

3 On contact do not create any wrist movement. Keep the clubhead low with the face at right angles to the ground. Your head position should stay very still and there is no leg or hip movement.

4 On these short putts it is tempting to look at the hole as you stroke the putt, but continue concentrating on the shot.

THE LONG PUTT

1 During the set-up for the longer putt think of the distance you have to roll the ball for it to reach the hole.

2 After impact keep your head still, stroke the ball smoothly towards the hole with the arms and club.

3 Even when the golf ball is halfway to the hole your head should still not have moved.

4 The only change in these two pictures has been the movement of the ball. The head has stayed still.

5 View of the follow-through. The putter reaching completion.

Key Points Card

Points	Remarks
1	Check you have the correct grip.
2	The ball should be aligned to the centre of the clubface.
3	The face of the club should be square to the target.
4	Putting is a shoulder and arms movement. There should be no wrist action during the stroke.
5	Keep your head still.

PUTTING PRACTICE

It is always best to practise on a level part of the green; once you can make the ball race straight on short distances then you will be able to cope with long putts and borrows in the greens.

The most important part of any putt is the first 9–12 ins (230–300 mm). If the shot starts correctly there is a good chance of success, but a putt that starts badly rarely improves.

Having lined the ball with the centre of the clubface practise making a smooth back and through swing striking the ball in the same spot – that is the spot on the clubface that you lined the ball up with at the address.

Depending on the speed and the length of the green the distance you have to swing the putter back will vary. For putts of up to 5–6 ins (125–150 mm) the putter head needs to go back in a straight line from the ball and hole. As the length of putt increases the length of the swing will also increase and in so doing the putter will come back slightly on the inside.

1 You do not need a hole to practise this exercise. Take four balls and play the first one to an open area.

2 Repeat the same putt three or more times, get the four balls to finish as close to one another as possible.

3 This exercise will help you practise the pace of the green and develop a consistent stroke.

HOLING SHORT PUTTS

Place four balls each a little further from the hole. Hole them, working from the one nearest to the hole. Start by testing yourself on a short putt and gradually move the balls further away.

SHAPING THE PUTT

The amount you have to allow for borrows on the greens will depend on the texture of the grass, which in turn determines the speed of the green. The golden rule is that if you decide that you have to allow for the ball to move left or right because of the lie of the land, then you must endeavour to set the ball moving straight from the putter head and let the ground shape the putt. If the surface of the green is fast then you need to allow more into the borrow.

Always look from behind the ball to see what shape the putt is going to make. If you are undecided then take a look at the putt from the hole back to the ball. On a downhill putt you will always see the line more clearly from the hole to the ball. When the putt is uphill have a good look from the side of the putt. This will give you a better view of the slope you are about to negotiate.

Key Points Card	
Points	**Remarks**
1	*Start by practising short putts to build up your confidence.*
2	*Repeat the same length of putt several times to develop a consistent stroke.*
3	*Then practise putts moving further away from the hole each time.*
4	*If there are borrows in the green let the ground shape the putt.*

THE ELEMENTS OF PUTTING

Address the ball with the face of the putter at right angles to the ground and the ball in line with your left heel. Strike the ball with an upward movement to cause top spin and roll. Keep the putter head quite low to the ground as it passes the left shoe. Having set your line and address you must stand quite still and stroke the ball and make it roll.

Opposite: Greg Norman.

HAZARDS AND DIFFICULT SHOTS

However good you are at golf there are bound
to be times when you will find yourself in an
awkward situation, whether it is under some
trees, on a slope or in a bunker. In these cases it
is often best not to be too ambitious, and you
should concentrate on the job in hand – getting
your ball back on to the fairway. Once there
you can think about your next shot.

GREENSIDE BUNKER

1 Feet, legs, hips and shoulders open to the target. Position the ball just left of the centre in your stance. This will help you to present the full loft of the club to the target. Settle your feet in the sand, this will give you a firm stance and help you feel its consistency. Look at the sand about 2 in (50 mm) behind the ball. Because of the open stance a little more of your lower body-weight will be on your left leg. Use the standard hold on the club so that the clubface is open to your stance.

2 Take the club back and up with your hands and arms, and a responding shoulder, hip and leg movement. The amount of movement required will depend on how far you have to hit the shot. Notice how the club that is swung back is pointing in the same direction as the club aligned along the feet. This indicates that the golf club should move along the line of the address position.

3 At the start of the downswing the clubhead has lots of loft and the face is visible. With this alignment and arm-swing, your swing should naturally go across the ball-to-target line. Keep your hands and arms together, working underneath the golf club.

4 Make contact with the sand about 2 in (50 mm) behind the ball. Head position very still. Move your legs and hips out of the way to help your shoulders keep the line they were set in at the address. The ball will move left of the target along the swing path of the club. But because you aimed the clubface at the target, and open to your stance, the ball will cut in its flight.

5 Your right leg, hip and shoulder move to help take the swing high on the follow-through. Keep your hold on the club and continue to swing along the open line set by your body at the address.

Key Points Card

Points	Remarks
1	Use a sand wedge with bounce.
2	Ball forward in the stance.
3	Look at the sand where you intend to hit.
4	Swing along the open shoulder line.
5	Follow through keeping loft on the clubface.

GREENSIDE BUNKER: EXAMPLE TWO

1 Ball slightly forward and clubhead above the sand.

2 This shows the swing of the hands and arms taking the club back and up.

3 Body swinging under the head, arms extended with the hands keeping the loft on the face of the club.

4 Hands held high with the shoulders just bringing the head around.

5 Body pointing left of the target with a full follow-through.

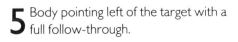

BALL BACK IN GREENSIDE BUNKER

1 Set the ball slightly left of centre in the stance and perhaps a little further away from your feet. Align your body to the left of the target.

2 Swing the club further back, making a fuller hip and shoulder turn. Make sure your arms and legs are working well together on the downswing. Wrists still cocked, head very still with plenty of room for the shoulders to move.

3 Less sand is taken. Your wrists and hands bring the loft of the club through the ball to send it high enough to cover the full distance of the sand.

4 Notice the high follow-through. Keep the top of your body tilted over the ground.

5 Turn your body completely to face to the left of the target and maintain your balance.

FRONT OF GREENSIDE BUNKER: BALL SAT DOWN

I Stand in a relaxed address position, feet slightly open, shoulders square, the clubhead square to your shoulders and do not hold the club too tightly.

2 Take the club back with your hands and arms, with a little movement coming from your shoulders and hips.

3 Swing down to hit the sand several inches behind the ball. It is likely that your hold on the club will tighten a little at this point.

4 Again head steady. You will hit lots of sand, but keep your arms and hands moving ahead of the golf club. This will ensure you do not turn the club over as you hit the sand.

BALL ON FIRM SAND IN GREENSIDE BUNKER

1 This shot will need a smooth full swing, not taking very much sand.

2 Take the club back without such an early wrist break. This will help get a shallower attack on the sand.

3 Relaxed body and arm-swing to the top of the backswing.

4 Slip the club under the ball slowly.

5 Good release of the clubhead.

6 Make a relaxed full follow-through.

BALL ON THE UP-SLOPE OF GREENSIDE BUNKER

1 Position the ball slightly to the left of centre in the stance. Set your body perpendicular to the slope. To achieve this you will need to widen the stance and flex your knees into the slope.

2 As with all these bunker shots keep your head steady.

3 Maintain your balance and the angles set at the address. Take the club back and up with your hands and arms.

4 Your legs should hold your body in to the slope. Swing the club to the ball with the top of your body.

5 Because your legs are working to hold your body on the slope, the hip movement through will be at a minimum causing a restricted follow-through.

BALL PLUGGED IN GREENSIDE BUNKER

1 Note how the clubface has been turned in to a closed position and at the same time the grip is correct. Your stance should be square, with the ball positioned centrally between your feet. Feet set firmly in the sand.

4 Work with your legs and hips keeping your arms down in a position ready to hit a lot of sand.

2 Look at the sand several inches behind the ball. Set off on a smooth full swing.

5 Lots of sand will be hit to get the clubhead down and under the ball. The weight of the sand will open the clubhead. This is why you set the clubface closed.

3 At the top of backswing make a good shoulder turn. The clubface has kept its closed position.

6 Make every effort to follow through, but this is often hard. On these occasions getting the ball out of the bunker is about the best that you can hope for.

BALL IN A FAIRWAY BUNKER

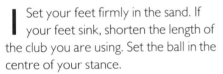

1 Set your feet firmly in the sand. If your feet sink, shorten the length of the club you are using. Set the ball in the centre of your stance.

2 As you take the clubhead up and away from the ball, look at the top of the ball and firm up your hold on the club. These points will help you take the ball more cleanly from the sand.

3 The firm hold on the club will restrict your wrist action. Take the club back with your body.

4 Full backswing, good shoulder turn and the club pointing parallel to the target as your body is set square to the ball-to-target line.

5 Your body-weight should be on your left side. Hands and arms ready to take the ball before you hit the sand.

7 A well-balanced follow-through and the arms are now folded.

6 Hold your head steady, take the ball quite cleanly off the sand. Your hands and arms release the club with your arms together as they were at address.

3 At impact you will first strike the ball, then a little sand. Swing the club past the body.

FAIRWAY BUNKER: EXAMPLE TWO

1 Embed your feet slightly into the sand to give a firm stance.

2 Your body and arms should be working together as you complete the backswing.

4 High follow-through, with your body facing the target.

Key Points Card

Points	Remarks
1	Choose the club that will give you enough loft to get over the lip of the bunker.
2	Keep a firm hold on the club.
3	Look at the top of the ball.
4	Make a smooth, balanced swing.

THE PROFESSIONALS

Nick Faldo of England playing from a greenside bunker. Here you can see clearly that the loft on the clubface has thrown the ball up and out of the bunker.

BALL ON AN UPHILL LIE

Do not be ambitious on sloping lies. The uphill lie is probably the least difficult but it is essential that you are well-balanced and that you work with the slopes rather than fighting them. The main thing you have to work out when playing on an uphill lie is how to make the clubhead swing down and up the slope. To do this you have to set your body at right angles to the hill. This will make the golf club more lofted, so select a less lofted club to start off with. Note the action you are going to make will tend to hook the ball, so aim right of your intended target.

1 In setting the angle of your spine at right angles to the slope bend your left leg slightly more than usual.

2 This will restrict the movement of your hips through impact and is likely to make your hands more active and inclined to cross over.

3 Play the ball off your higher leg, that is your left leg; this will help in setting your spinal angle and will give you room to swing the clubhead down and up the slope.

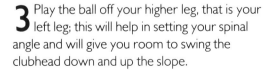

4 The angle that the body was set to the slope at the address has been maintained.

Key Points Card

Points	Remarks
1	*The club you select will depend on the severity of the slope and how you have to stand to control your balance.*
2	*Remember that both hands work together.*
3	*Hold the grip firmly with the last three fingers of the right hand.*
4	*Play the ball off your left (the higher) leg.*

BALL ON A DOWNHILL LIE

The downhill lie is probably the most difficult of all the hazardous shots that you will have to play. When playing all awkward lies you must always play within your limits and not be too ambitious. First work out where you want the ball to come to rest. In the set-up stand so that it is possible to swing the club up and down the slope. You have to position the ball back from the centre of your stance and incline your body down the slope to make your spine vertical to the angle of the ball. Doing this will cancel the angle of loft on the clubface so it is important that you take a more lofted club than normal. Club selection will depend on the severity of the slope.

1 Position the ball back from the centre of the stance.

2 You will now be bent into the slope and it will be difficult to make a complete body turn. Therefore, this is a hand and arm shot. The backswing will not be as complete as normal.

3 To take the ball cleanly off the ground keep the club low to the ground as it goes through impact.

4 Make every effort to keep your hands ahead of the clubhead when striking the ball. This will ensure the leading edge is square and that the clubhead moves down the slope.

5 Make a shortened follow-through and the ball should fly away low and straight.

BALL BELOW YOUR FEET

When the ball is below your feet the tendency is for the body to fall forward causing the backswing to go back on an upright plane and the hands to roll the clubface open. Consequently, you are likely to cut across the ball with an open face, sending the golf ball off swerving from left to right. As you will see from the following pictures the best way to play this shot will result in the ball flying high and only a short distance. You must accept this, rather than trying to gain extra distance through playing a more ambitious shot.

1 In the address position ensure that you use the full length of the golf club. Hold the grip near the end of the shaft.

2 Set the golf ball forward in your stance. Aim left of your target. Put more weight on your heels to avoid falling down the slope.

3 On the takeaway do not fight the slope. Use less body movement, and swing with your hands and arms.

4 Keep your balance as you hit the shot, let the club come down to impact with an open face.

5 Do not try and close it – this will result in you falling down the slope and fluffing the shot. Your follow-through will be restricted.

BALL ABOVE YOUR FEET

When the ball is above your feet the tendency is for the ball to hook. This is due to the fact that when you place the club to the ball the clubface will be facing to the left of your target. Also with the ball above your feet your swing plane becomes flatter.

1 Aim to the right of your intended target.

2 Hold the grip of the club several inches down from the top. If you use the full length of the club you risk hitting the ground before the ball. Set your body-weight into the slope to prevent falling backwards when you swing the club back and through.

3 The swing must be a smooth body and arm movement, without a lot of hand action.

4 This shows how the arm-swing has been flattened by the lie of the ball above the feet.

5 At impact, because of the danger of the slope, play with a lot of hand action. But note this closes the face of the club severely causing the shot to be smothered.

6 Well-balanced, with a flat follow-through showing how the club and swing accommodate the slope.

Key Points Card

Points	Remarks
1	*Play with the ball in the middle of your stance.*
2	*Hold down the grip several inches.*
3	*Aim slightly right of the target to allow for the hook.*
4	*Set your balance into the slope.*
5	*The angle of the slope will cause a flatter swing plane and path. Do not resist this.*
6	*Keep the swing smooth.*

HIGH SHOTS OVER TREES

You may find yourself in the unfortunate position of having to play this rather awkward shot. In cases such as these it often pays not to be too ambitious and to work on getting the ball back into a playing position. In this case the ball has missed the fairway to the left and there are some large trees in the way. Club selection is of great importance. You will need some distance but the most important consideration is to have enough height to clear the trees. Each time you play an awkward shot like this, take time to imagine the flight line you require.

1 Set the ball forward in your stance, make sure your grip pressure is not too tight and think hard about the shot you are going to make.

2 At impact your shoulders should be very square helping to keep the loft on the clubface and your head well back to give an upward strike on the ball. Here the ball can be seen setting off in an upward lift.

3 See how the whole movement suggests the ball is being hit forward and up into the air. The ball has been taken cleanly off the ground.

4 Remain well-balanced, holding your body under the shot, turn your head and look underneath the ball.

LOW SHOTS IN BUSHES

I If you need to restrict the uplift of the club on the backswing separate your hands from one another. Exactly how far apart you place them will depend on how far back you can take the club. You may need to bend your body low to get under the branches. Position the ball back in the stance which will make impact earlier.

DIFFICULT SHOTS

When the ball has to be lofted quickly, for example over a mound or out of a deep bunker, set the clubface open.

When you follow through playing from a greenside bunker or any high shot, hit through the ball and keep the loft on the club.

2 See here how the arms take the club back and the body-weight remains still. All these points help to avoid hitting the branches.

3 Impact is made with the right hand and arms, and the head is kept very still. The ball is now out and on to the fairway for the next shot.

LOW SHOTS UNDER TREES

1 Position the ball slightly back in the stance but make sure the left hand is still in line with the inside of your left leg. The head of the club will be slightly hooded if the leading edge is square to the target line. Flex your right leg inwards at the knee, which will settle your weight slightly on to your left side.

2 Swing the club back and up with your arms and hands. The legs and hips make very little movement and, therefore, your weight should not move to the right.

3 Keep your head still as your arms and legs pull the club down to the ball. Your hips should be square to the target line and your shoulders still back.

4 Keep your body low and punch the ball away with your forearms. Notice the left wrist position, this helps to take the loft off the club and keep the ball low.

EXAMPLE TWO

1 This shows the same shot but from behind the ball. From this position you can see how the ball must fly low.

2 The shoulders move to help the arms take the club back and the legs are flexed keeping a solid base to the swing.

3 The hands maintain a firm hold of the club, arms working closely together.

4 The right shoulder moves down and through.

Key Points Card

Points	Remarks
1	Ball back slightly in the address.
2	Keep the leading edge of the club square, deloft (hood) the club.
3	As you strike the ball keep your hands and arms ahead of the club.
4	Keep your head still.

THE PROFESSIONALS

Sandy Lyle of Scotland having to punch the ball out of heavy rough with a lofted club. You can see here that he is using an interlocking grip.

Opposite: Ian Woosnam

FAULTS AND PROBLEM SOLVING

If a golf ball is hit correctly it will fly straight towards the target. Shots that deviate to the left or right have been wrongly struck. The faults can be many and may be in your aim, your grip, your stance and your swing. In this chapter the pictures with pink shirts are the ones where errors are being shown and the white shirts show the correct action.

SLICING

The slice is a ball that swings from left to right in its flight. As you will see from the pictures below the slice is caused by an open address position. This leads to an out-to-in swing path and the clubface being open to this swing path. The ball starts off flying on the swing path – to the left – but the open clubface puts spin on the ball and so it swerves round to the right. It is the swing path that directs the ball and the shape of the clubface at impact that spins the ball.

In the following pictures the clubs on the ground indicate parallel lines to the centre of the fairway, highlighting the open stance. In most cases players are not aware that they are making this error and they will still make an effort in the swing to send the clubface and ball to the fairway.

Always aim correctly for every shot. When you start with problems at the address the chances of making the correct back and through swing are made more difficult.

FRONT VIEW

1 Open set-up. The ball is a long way forward in the stance and the head is over the ball. Because of the open set-up the 'V's on both hands are pointing to the left shoulder which will cause an opening of the clubface during the swing.

2 The forward position of the ball and the open shoulders have restricted the shoulder turn. The club is now pointing left with the face open.

3 At impact the body is open. The hands are forward and the club is open to the body.

4 The club is travelling on the inside. The head is well forward, but there has been no release of the clubhead.

5 The follow-through is well left of the fairway and the clubhead is being held open by the hands.

SLICING: EXAMPLE TWO

1 This gives a clear view of a very open stance and alignment. The clubs on the ground indicate parallel lines to the centre of the fairway. In most cases the golfer is not aware he is making this error which leads to attempts to compensate in the swing in order to hit the ball straight.

2 Because of the open address, the arms have swung the club to the left of the target. In doing this the club was taken back on the outside and is now all set to swing down on the outside.

3 At impact, the shoulders and hips turn to the left of the target taking the arms inside the ball-to-target line. In attempting to hit the ball to the target the hands have now turned the clubface open to the swing path.

4 The clubhead moves through impact onto the inside path. The clubface is open. Therefore, the ball will start flying left because this is the direction of the swing path, but the open clubface puts spin on the ball, so it will swerve to the right once it is in its flight.

5 The head and shoulders are now well forward. The hands have not released the clubhead. The body is facing well left of the fairway.

PULLING

A pull is a shot that sends the ball flying straight to the left. It has the same swing path as the slice – out-to-in – but a different shaped clubhead at impact. The clubface is square at impact.

1 Notice how the set-up is the same as the set-up for the slice.

2 The swing is along the line of the body. As far as the target is concerned this golf club is 'laid off' – pointing to the left of the target. On the downswing the club will travel on the outside.

3 In the downswing you can see the club is about to travel down on the outside.

4 After impact the club is well over to the left, covering the ground called the inside. The ball is going to the left but stays straight because at impact the hands squared the clubface to this out-to-in swing path.

5 The follow-through shows that the clubhead was released along the out-to-in swing path.

HOOKING

A hook is the opposite shot to the slice, it sends the ball from right to left. The swing path is in-to-out, so the ball starts to the right following the swing path, but because the clubhead is closed at impact the ball spins round to the left. The hook is caused by errors in the set-up which in turn affect the swing plane and swing path.

1 Here the whole alignment is facing well to the right of the centre of the fairway, showing a closed stance. This is opposite to the slice. On the takeaway the club will travel on the inside.

2 At the top of the backswing the club is pointing along the closed shoulder line, to the right of the target. This is known as being 'across the line'. The clubhead is closing; the clubface is facing the sky.

3 The downswing comes in very much on the inside, keeping the right side well back.

4 The club is moving on a swing path to the outside. The ball starts going to the right but because the hands turned the clubhead over, in an attempt to hit the ball to the target, the ball will spin off to the left.

5 The body is in the way so the arms are struggling to make a proper follow-through.

FLIGHT PATHS

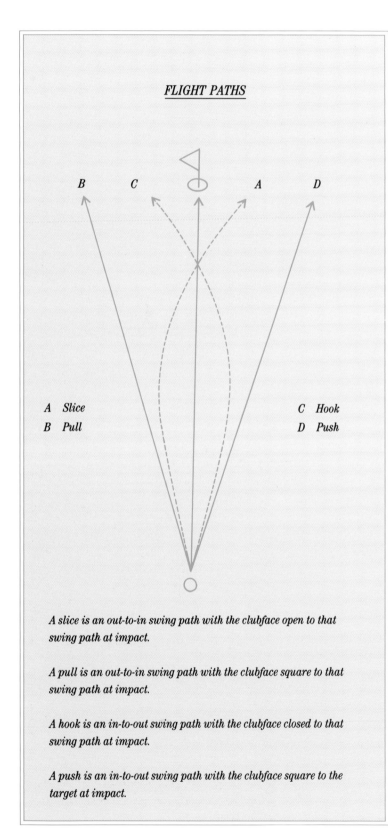

A Slice
B Pull
C Hook
D Push

A slice is an out-to-in swing path with the clubface open to that swing path at impact.

A pull is an out-to-in swing path with the clubface square to that swing path at impact.

A hook is an in-to-out swing path with the clubface closed to that swing path at impact.

A push is an in-to-out swing path with the clubface square to the target at impact.

FRONT VIEW

1 The ball is set back in the address. The feet, knees, hips and shoulders are aiming to the right of the target. Therefore, both 'V's are pointing more to the right shoulder.

2 As the club reaches the top of the backswing, notice the closed clubface and how the club points across the line of the club on the ground.

THE PROFESSIONALS

Severiano Ballesteros of Spain recovering from a hook into rough grass. With his swashbuckling style Ballesteros is a master at dealing with awkward lies and bunkers.

3 The ball is hit from the inside. The right shoulder is well back and not helping the club to move through impact.

4 The hands have turned the face over causing the hook. The ball will swerve to the left.

5 The fact that the right side was not helping the club through at impact shows now in the follow-through.

PUSHING

A push is the opposite shot to the pull, it sends the ball flying straight to the right. It has the same swing path as the hook – in-to-out – so the ball starts to the right, but because the clubhead is square to the swing path at impact the ball does not have spin on it, and stays straight in its flight path.

1 Once again the alignment is facing well to the right of the centre of the fairway. This is a closed stance.

2 At the top of backswing the club is pointing across the line and the clubface is closed.

3 This results in the attack on the ball being too much from the inside.

4 Impact is in-to-out and the clubface is square to the swing path. The ball starts right and flies straight along this line. Because the clubface was square at impact there is no side spin on the ball.

5 The ball was hit straight down the right side of the course.

PUSHING: EXAMPLE TWO

1 The set-up is facing to the right of target. The ball is well back in the stance, so the takeaway will go back quickly on the inside. This shot could be either a hook or a push.

3 The swing path is on the inside and the clubface is square to this path. The shot is a push. The ball will fly straight to the right.

2 The club closes at the top of the backswing. The shot could still be a hook or a push.

4 Because of the in-to-out swing path, the body is in the way of the follow-through and cannot clear.

TOPPING

This is the type of mistake that you are inclined to make when you are starting to play golf and have not learned to trust your movements. In the following examples note how the upward action has been made either with the body or the clubhead. This is incorrect as it is the loft on the face of the club that sends the ball in the air. In each case the position of the legs at the address, and how they work to turn the body and aid weight transference throughout the shot, need to be improved.

1 At the address the set-up is square and the posture is good. Everything looks ready for the backswing.

2 The club was swung to a good position by the hands and arms, but as you can see the legs have straightened causing the angle of the posture to rise. If the angle of the spine is not reset at this stage the club will hit the top half of the ball.

3 Just before impact. Sadly the legs and back have not recovered the angles that were set at the address. The hands and arms are trying to find the ball, but it is now too late, the top is imminent.

4 Everything except the ball is going up.

TOPPING: EXAMPLE TWO

1 The feet are a little closed and shoulders just a touch open. The head position is not set for a good shoulder pivot.

2 The head has to move to the right to allow for the shoulder turn. This causes the body to sway to the right as the arms and hands go back and up.

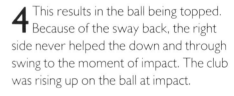

3 The hands and arms are bringing the club to the ball, but the body is still far back on the right leg.

4 This results in the ball being topped. Because of the sway back, the right side never helped the down and through swing to the moment of impact. The club was rising up on the ball at impact.

TOPPING: EXAMPLE THREE

1 All is set for the ball to be smashed straight down the middle, but the legs are possibly a little straight.

2 By now the legs are rather bent causing a loss of height, but a top could still be avoided. It might be possible to recover the position back to how it was at the address.

3 As the club is coming down to the impact area the body is moving up again, but there is still a chance of striking the ball in the correct place.

4 But the legs have straightened again, causing the top.

FLUFFING

The fluff is a shot where the club hits the ground before it hits the ball. It can occur with any type of shot at any time. As with topping, the problems often arise because of an incorrect position at the address. Always remember to check your alignment, stance and posture before you start the takeaway.

1 The address is looking good except that the golf ball is too far back in the stance. This may mean that the body-weight is incorrectly distributed at the start of the swing.

2 At the top of the backswing you can see that the hands and arms have taken the club back in a very upright manner. There has been little to no weight transferred to the right side.

3 On the downswing you can see the result of the ball being too far back in the stance combined with the upright arm movement on the backswing. The head is now too far forward, leaving no room to get a clean strike at the ball.

4 The arms did their best to get the clubhead to the ball but because of the steepness of the angle of attack the clubhead hit the ground.

FLUFFING: EXAMPLE TWO

1 The stance is a little closed which means the ball will be too far back.

2 The club has been swung back outside the ball-to-target line, therefore creating an upright position at the top of the backswing.

3 The address position and backswing make it difficult to take the ball cleanly off the tee. This picture shows clearly how the bottom of the swing arrived too early, hence the amount of ground being moved.

4 This results in a restricted follow-through. Due to the upright arm-swing in the takeaway only the arms create the follow-through.

FLUFFING: EXAMPLE THREE

1 Once again you can see the address with the wood. The ball is teed-up correctly, but the shoulders are set slightly open to the feet and hips.

2 Because the top half of the body has lifted the club up to the top of the backswing, the right leg is very straight and the angle of the spine has been altered from the address.

3 On the downswing, the legs and body make a great effort to return to the level set at the address so that the ball can be taken off the tee.

4 Even though the recovery effort went on right into impact, the body continued to go down and the club could only hit the ground in front of the ball.

OVER-SWINGING

The over-swing is a common error. Whilst you notice it mainly at the top of the backswing, the next set of pictures demonstrate that the faults can actually be seen right at the beginning of the swing. First, look at the incorrect swings. Then compare them to the correct swing.

ARM-SWING AND BODY TURN AT THE START OF THE SWING

1 The club is well on its way to the backswing. It has clearly been taken back with virtually no help from the body. The clubhead has moved much more than any other part. As a result the left arm has started to bend at the elbow. The club was taken back too far, too fast, too soon.

2 At the top of the backswing, in spite of making some movement the body has not caught up with the club. Now, the left arm is a little more bent, the arms are further apart, and the head and shaft of the club have gone beyond the horizontal line.

3 You can see clearly how the arms separated at the top of the backswing. At this stage recovery can still be made but it will be difficult to produce a consistent shot.

4 Notice the splayed formation of the arms on the follow-through which suggests that the complete recovery was not made.

ERROR: EXAMPLE TWO

1 The ball and clubhead were set on the ball-to-target line at the address, with the feet, hips and shoulders parallel to this line. The body is making a good pivoting movement, but the arms and club have come up to join the body. Because of this the club moved slightly inside the ball-to-target line.

2 This shows the same action but from the front. Despite the good body movements the arms have brought the club up flat to the body losing the alignment to the target.

ERROR: EXAMPLE THREE

1 Again the clubhead and ball were set square to the target at the address. But only the arms have taken the club up, and in so doing it has gone slightly on the outside of the ball-to-target line. With this arm-swing, the body is moving along the ball-to-target line instead of pivoting.

2 This shows the same action but from the front. The body has moved sideways and the head and shoulders are down. This is an arm-swing without the correct body turn.

THE CORRECT SWING

The first picture shows the start of the backswing from an address position that was square to the ball-to-target line. The clubhead and shaft have been taken to about waist height with a turning movement of the left shoulder, left hip and a swinging movement of the left arm and the whole of the club. The right shoulder, right arm and right hip have in no way stopped the left side making this movement. The head position is held steady, the pressure of the hands on the club maintained, the right leg is still flexed as it was in the address.

Take note that the hands and the face of the club have worked together without any independent wrist movement, also that the left arm and the club are now parallel to the ball-to-target line. This one-piece movement has brought the club slightly on the inside of the target line.

If at this stage you were to look at your hold on the grip you would see that the 'V'-shapes of your hands were still pointing between your face and right shoulder, as they were at the address.

This second picture shows the same position but from the front. Because the club and the left side have moved to the right some weight has been transferred on to the instep of the right foot. The right leg has kept its position which will create the hip turn. The position of the head and spinal angle have been maintained, promoting the correct turn and tilt of the shoulders. The arms and club have remained the same distance apart as they were at the address.

Again you can see how the hands and clubface have moved together. Controlling the shape of the clubhead and its direction at the start of the backswing is of great importance. This is a one-piece takeaway.

Opposite: Fred Couples.

ERRORS IN THE SHORT GAME

Although pitching, chipping and putting are all part of the short game, the elements of these shots are the same as for full shots – you want the ball to end up where you have aimed it. As such some of the errors are similar to those discussed in the previous chapter, but these shots also present their own problems, not least the problem of dealing with pressure.

The pictures with pink shirts are the ones where errors are being shown and the white or blue shirts show the correct action.

ERRORS IN PITCHING

The pitch is a shot that is used to hit the ball straight and in the air. Therefore, you must first select a club with loft on it such as a 9-iron, wedge or sand wedge. These will give you the height on the shot that you need. As in all shots, for the pitch you start by lining up the leading edge of the club square to the target. It should be at right angles to the ball-to-target line.

Three types of errors are shown below. Firstly, topping, otherwise known as thinning. Secondly, fluffing, otherwise known as hitting the ball flat. This is when you hit the ground before you hit the ball. Thirdly, there is the socket. This dreadful shot is when you hit the ball with the heel of the club and is commonly known as a shank.

TOPPING

1 It is tempting to imagine that leaning back on the right leg, with the hands back, will lift the ball up and over the bunker. But this ignores the fact that it is the loft on the club that sends the ball into the air.

2 In this address position the club will be taken back with the hands and wrists holding on to the club, not letting the wrists cock. Also see how the head has moved to the left, perhaps with the idea that it should be kept down.

3 Contact is made with the leading edge of the club so the ball is hit into the bunker. See how all the effort seems to be going into lifting the ball up in the air. The head is to the right, the hands have stopped and the clubhead is up in the air, causing impact to be halfway up the side of the ball. The left heel is off the ground, which is helping to make a lifting action.

4 This detail shows the position of the club at impact. There is no loft on this part of the club. You should strike the ball in the centre of the clubface.

5 In the completed swing the body is well back, with the left foot more off the ground and the arms and hands still trying to lift the ball over the bunker.

FLUFFING

1 The miscalculation here is the belief that if you take a lofted club and hit down at the ball it will go into the air. This explains why the ball is so far back in the stance and the body-weight and head so far forward. In truth, standing like this will probably take loft off the clubface.

2 The club is taken up and back quite severely with the hands and arms. You can see more clearly here how far ahead of the ball the player is standing.

3 In the picture you can see very clearly that the ground has been hit before the ball. The ball is airborne but it will not make the distance required because it was hit too far up the clubface. This part of the club does not propel the ball forward with any speed.

4 Due to the steep angle of attack, the follow-through is very restricted. This is a good example of the loft on the clubface not being used correctly.

THE SOCKET

1 Notice how the hands and arms have taken the club back too far on the inside of the ball-to-target line.

2 The wrists are too cocked, taking the club too far back. If the clubhead is brought straight down from this position the swing path will be in-to-out, and the ball will fly to the right.

3 Here though, instead of swinging in-to-out, an attempt is made to correct the backswing. The shoulders have turned but at impact the clubhead is slightly further away from the body. The heel of the club, the socket, collides with the ball.

4 This picture illustrates the position of the clubhead at impact.

5 The body has come up because the club and arms swung out and around on the downswing, and at impact.

CORRECT PITCH

1 Comfortable address, clubhead and ball aiming at the target.

2 Hands and arms take the club straight back and up.

3 Impact, then the club and arms swing towards the flag.

4 The right side helps the movement to the target.

5 The weight is on the left side in a well-balanced follow-through.

ERRORS IN CHIPPING

The chip is a shot that can be played with the putter if the ground between the ball and the green is clean and fast. The chip must travel straight and on a low trajectory because it is a running shot. As in pitching, once you have selected the stroke you intend to play, you must not change your mind. Judging the distance on these shots can only come from plenty of practice. When chipping you must avoid opening and closing the clubhead during the swing. The stroke needs to be played without wrist action so that the clubhead can be kept close to the ground throughout the playing of the shot. It is very similar to the putt. The following pictures show a couple of common errors.

1 The medium iron has been selected and the address position is looking good – slightly more weight on the left leg, clubface a little hooded to help the ball run, and hands down the grip to reduce the size of the backswing.

2 This is where the mistake occurs. There appears to have been a change of plan – the hands and wrists have taken the clubhead back into an open position. This is the action you would use if you intended to play a lofted shot.

3 At impact, the hands roll the clubface back to the ball closing the head and overcompensating for the open face on the backswing. This is seen clearly by the position of the right hand and the shape of the clubhead.

4 The clubhead continues in this rolling manner sending the ball too far and to the left.

ERROR: EXAMPLE TWO

I The ball is lying well on the fairway, just short of the apron of the green. A medium iron has been chosen for this chip and run shot. At the address the hands are too far back and behind the ball, which will cause the clubhead to be more lofted than is necessary. Also the body-weight is incorrect. It should set slightly more on the left leg than the right.

2 On the backswing, note how the clubhead has not stayed low to the ground but has been picked up by the hands. The clubface now has too much loft on it for this shot.

3 Partly because the body-weight is too central only the right hand and arm have been used to bring the club to the impact area. See how the left hand, head and arm have stopped, causing the clubhead to rise when it strikes the ball and, therefore, topping it.

4 Further on through the shot, the clubhead is a long way from the ground. The left hand and arm stopped when the strike was made. On this occasion the ball will probably shoot right across the green, no doubt finishing in some trouble.

CORRECT CHIP

Remember when you want a low shot, keep the clubhead low to the ground on both the back and the through swing, making every effort to ensure that the arms and club move as far forward through the shot as they moved back on the backswing.

1 Hands down the grip; leading edge square; well-balanced address.

2 Just before impact the body is still and the left hand and shaft together. Clubhead delofted.

3 At impact the arms and club return together to the ball. The clubhead is low to the ground.

4 Now the ball is on its way, flying low. The club, hands and arms have moved together, and in so doing, have kept the clubhead low to the ground.

5 The body is well-balanced, the ball is about to land and then roll up to the target, the flag.

ERRORS IN PUTTING

If you are to make the ball roll into the hole on the putting green successfully then you must make sure that the ball starts along the correct line. The following pictures illustrate some of the common errors which cause disappointment on the green. Remember that you must align the ball with the centre of the clubhead, and set the ball in a position that enables you to take the putter back smoothly, low to the ground. The fewer movements you make with your hands and wrists when taking the clubhead backwards and forwards, the better.

1 The ball is lined up with the toe of the putter. This may cause the ball to roll to the right, and very often short, of the hole.

2 The golf ball is in line with the heel of the putter. This will hit the ball left of the target. From this point on the club it is also hard to make the ball roll smoothly.

Here the body is set square to the hole, but the head is not over the line of the putt. The hands are also a little low, with the ball too far away.

2 The hands and arms have taken the putter back from the ball, outside the ball-to-hole line. A good putting action would have taken the putter back along the ball-to-hole line. On a longer putt it would have gone slightly on the inside.

3 Just before impact, you can see the putter head on the line of the target. The ball will be struck with the heel of the putter.

4 The putter head is well to the left of the hole, the hands have tried to square up the clubface. This action is responsible for a lot of missed putts from all lengths.

ERROR: EXAMPLE TWO

1 The set-up appears to be aiming to the right of the hole, with the golf ball displaced towards the toe of the putter. The tendency from here is to swing the putter head back too much on the inside of the line.

2 As the putter head is just about to make contact, see how the putter face is now aiming very much to the right, so the clubface is open to the hole. As this is a level putt and there is no need to allow for any slope on the green there is not much chance of the ball rolling towards the hole.

3 The ball is away. You can see clearly that the swing of the putter head back and through was in no way able to send the ball to the hole.

4 The ball continues to move away from the hole.

2 The result of this address position is that the action at the start of the stroke is made by the wrists. They almost pick the putter head up.

ERROR: EXAMPLE THREE

1 The golf ball is a long way back in the stance. Therefore, the face of the putter cannot be at right angles to the ground and the leading edge of the putter will be tilted sharply into the putting surface.

THE PROFESSIONALS

Bernhard Langer of Germany having missed a putt at Kiawah, South Carolina, during the 1991 Ryder Cup. This tragedy at the final hole cost the European team the trophy.

3 The putter head comes down to the ball with the action being made by the hands and wrists.

4 The putter head will then hit the ground as it strikes the ball and come to a stop.

ERROR: EXAMPLE FOUR

1 See here how the shaft of the putter comes straight up, the forearms splay out and the elbows are bent. Having set this angle for the shaft of the club and the arms, it must be kept the same if you are to make a smooth stroke.

2 But as the putter went back the hands went forward to the hole. This changes the way the arms are set compared to their position at the address. The shaft and the left arm are now in line with one another.

3 An effort has been made to take the left hand and arm back to their position in the address. Now the right arm and the putter are in line.

4 The whole action is loose and wristy causing very poor contact on the ball.

ERROR: EXAMPLE FIVE

1 Everything appears to be going well. The putter is going back low to the ground. Hands, arms and putter moving together, no wrist break.

2 The putter has reached the right point in the backswing for this length of putt. But what you cannot see on looking at this picture is that the golfer can see the hole out of the corner of his left eye.

3 The moment the ball was played the player started to look at the hole, causing the shoulders to turn and brake the forward momentum of the clubhead towards the hole.

4 Now he will have to will the ball to keep moving.

ERROR: EXAMPLE SIX

1&2 Again the error here is that the head has moved. Practise these short putts keeping your head still and listening for the ball to go into the hole.

3 Here you can see that the head is still with the shoulders square.

ERROR: EXAMPLE SEVEN

1–3 Here the head has kept still but far too much hand and wrist action has been used.

4 Here the hands, arms and putter are all working together.

RULES AND ETIQUETTE

HANDICAPS

Handicapping is a system whereby strokes are subtracted from the scores of weaker players to enable golfers of different standards to compete fairly against one another. Handicaps are issued by golf clubs and authorized amateur golf associations.

HANDICAP ALLOWANCES

MATCH-PLAY
In match-play the handicap allowance is worked out as ¾ of the difference between the players handicaps. For example, if player A is a 25 handicap and player B is a 10 handicap, the difference is 15. Three-quarters of 15 is 11¼, therefore, player A receives 11 strokes. These are taken at the holes where the figure 11 and under appears on the stroke index on the score card. If the difference does not come out to a whole number it is rounded up.

STROKE-PLAY (MEDAL-PLAY)
In stroke-play you must complete every hole, then the whole handicap is deducted from the total score of the 18 holes completed. If the total score is 90, less a handicap of 15, the score is 75.

SINGLE STABLEFORD
The allowance for single stableford is ⅞ths of the total handicap. For example, if the player has a handicap of 19, ⅞ths of 19 is 16.625, this is rounded up to 17. These strokes are taken at the holes where 17 and below are shown on the stroke index.

FOUR BALL MATCH-PLAY
Each player receives ¾ of the difference in handicap taken from the lowest handicap of the four players. The strokes are taken at the holes indicated on the stroke index.

FOURSOME MATCH-PLAY
In foursome match-play, add together the handicap of each partnership.

FOURSOME STABLEFORD
Each pairing receives ⁷⁄₁₆ of their combined handicap; these strokes are taken at the holes indicated on the stroke index.

FOURSOME STROKE-PLAY
Each pairing receives ½ of their combined handicap, this is then taken from their gross score for the completed 18 holes.

Fred Couples and his caddy approaching the green at the Masters, 1992. Caddies are amongst other things responsible for the care of the equipment and measuring distances. Some players build up a strong relationship with their caddy, keeping the same one for years.

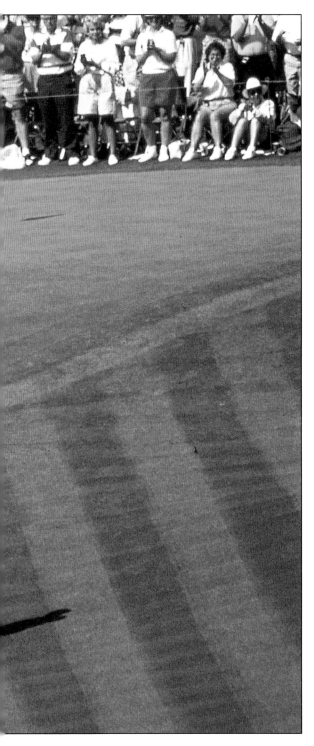

FOURSOME STABLEFORD BETTER-BALL

Each player receives ⅞ths of their handicap. These strokes are taken at the holes indicated on the stroke index. The better ball of the two players is the score for each hole. Total points recorded is the team score.

FOUR BALL BETTER-BALL STROKE-PLAY

Each player receives ¾ of their handicap. Each pair then records their best gross and nett score for each hole, using the stroke index, the best nett score on each hole will be the pairings score.

Golf is a game of world-wide popularity. This is the 18th green and clubhouse at Monastir, Tunisia.

RULES

There are a universal set of rules for golf that are constantly reviewed in Scotland by the Royal and Ancient Golf Club of St Andrews and in America by the United States Golf Association. Outlined below are some of the most important rules, but always check to see if a club has any special local rules of its own.

A modern set of irons.

STARTING OUT

Before play commences announce to your opponent the number and make of the ball you are going to start with.

You are only permitted to have fourteen clubs in your bag. They do not have to be different clubs, you can have two putters, several different wedges and sand wedges. It is the maximum number of fourteen that is important. Penalties are incurred for carrying more clubs and they are given regardless of the number of extra clubs. For stroke-play two penalty strokes are given on each hole on which the violation occurred, with a maximum penalty of four strokes. In match-play you lose the hole on which the violation occurred, with a maximum penalty per round of the loss of two holes. When playing stableford deduct two points from the final tally for each hole on which a violation occurred, maximum deduction four points.

THE HONOUR
Who is going to hit the ball first? This is called the honour. If it is an organized competition the honour is taken by the player whose name appears first for that game. Otherwise decide by tossing a coin.

THE TEEING GROUND
This is a flat prepared area, which will have two tee markers on it. These are usually stuck in the ground and can easily be moved by the ground staff to a different part of the tee to save wear on any one place. The tee of the day is a rectangle extending back two club lengths from a line between the markers. The ball must be teed-up within this area although you may stand outside it if you wish.

In match-play if you tee-up from outside the teeing ground your opponent can recall the shot played and ask you to take it again.

There is no penalty. In stroke-play you are penalized by two strokes and must then play from within the teeing ground. Strokes played from outside the teeing ground do not count. If you fail to return to the tee before you tee-off on the next hole, or leave the 18th green you are disqualified.

BALL FALLING OFF THE TEE PEG

This happens quite frequently. Even if the ball is teed-up in the correct way it may fall off of the tee at the address, or you might touch it with the clubhead and knock it off the tee. There is no penalty for this. Replace the ball on the tee peg and play away. However, if you have started your downswing when the ball topples from the tee and you are unable to check before impact, making a glancing blow on the ball or even missing it, this counts as a stroke. You cannot replace the ball on the tee peg. Should you be able to stop your downswing this does not constitute a stroke.

BALL IN PLAY

Once the game has begun the ball must be played as it lies, which means that you cannot touch it or improve its lie during the play to the green. Some courses do have a local rule which permits you to move the ball. This is often the case during the winter when the preferred lie rule can be introduced. The preferred lie rule entitles you to pick up the ball and replace it within 6 in (152 mm) of its original position, but it cannot be placed closer to the hole. If the ball comes to rest in casual water, it has to be dropped in accordance with the rules.

During the playing of each hole you are not permitted to play any practice strokes. A stroke is defined as the forward movement of the club with the intention of striking the ball. It is quite in order to have practice swings, but when doing this do not cause damage to the turf, also do not hold up play.

Pressing down the ground behind the ball, improving its lie, is not allowed at anytime once the ball is in play.

Below: Leaves and twigs being moved from around the ball. This is quite in order as long as you do not move the ball, but the items that are moved must be dead. You cannot break off any vegetation that is growing.

PLAYING THE WRONG BALL

Always make sure the ball you are about to play is your own; should you play the wrong ball you incur penalties. In match-play, you lose the hole. In stroke-play, add a two-stroke penalty and then play your own ball. If the ball you played belongs to a fellow competitor it must be replaced. The penalties do not apply if you are playing in a hazard.

LOST BALL

If your ball is lost you are allowed five minutes to look for it. Whenever this happens always tell the match behind you to play through. In match- and stroke-play, if after five minutes you cannot find the ball go back to where you played your last shot. If it was on the tee, tee-up a new ball, and if it was on the fairway or in the rough drop a new ball as near as possible to the spot where you played your last stroke. Add a penalty shot and lose the distance the ball went, for example, if your ball is lost from the tee shot your next shot will be counted as your third. This is known as stroke and distance.

BALL UNFIT FOR PLAY

If the ball is visibly damaged, by a cut or a crack, or has gone out of shape so that its true flight or roll is affected you can replace it without penalty. Make sure you consult with your opponent or marker. This does not apply for mud stuck to the side of the ball or if the paint is scratched.

BALL OUT OF BOUNDS

As with the lost ball, you apply the stroke and distance rule. Go back to where you played your last shot and add a penalty shot. Check the score card for out of bounds areas. It is the club's duty to define its boundaries. You can stand out of bounds to hit a ball that is in bounds.

DROPPING THE BALL

Stand upright and hold the ball at shoulder height. Drop the ball. If the ball touches you before it hits the ground it must be redropped, and you do not incur a penalty. You can be facing in any direction when dropping the ball.

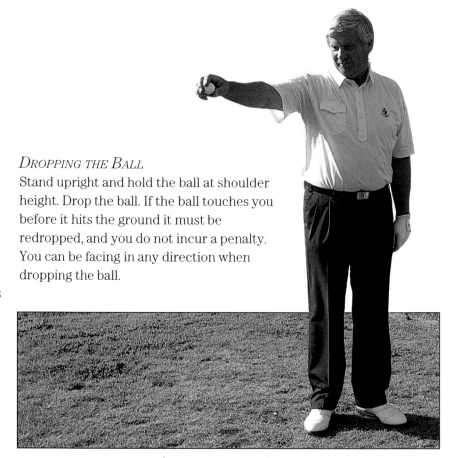

HAZARDS

GROUND UNDER REPAIR

This is an area where course maintenance is going on and will be clearly marked, often with a sign stating G.U.R. If your ball is in this area drop it clear at the nearest point of relief without penalty.

CASUAL WATER

If water is visible as you take your stance when playing through the green you are entitled to a free drop. This must be taken at the nearest point which avoids these conditions. It may mean your ball is on the fairway but the nearest point is in the rough – bad luck. Having determined the nearest point of relief drop the ball within one club-length of that point.

BUNKERS

A bunker is an area of bare ground most often a depression, which is usually covered in sand. The grass-covered banks of a bunker are not part of the bunker. Bunkers can be found anywhere on the golf course but mainly they are situated around the green.

When playing a stroke out of a bunker you must not ground the club in the sand when addressing the ball. Neither can you touch the sand on the backswing. Remember you cannot touch the sand in a bunker, or the ground in a hazard before you play a stroke. The penalty for this is two strokes in stroke play and loss of a hole in match-play. Always rake the bunker after you have played out to ensure the surface is smooth for the next unfortunate player to follow you there.

Opposite: When dropping the ball on the course, stand upright and hold the ball at shoulder height.

You must not ground the club into the sand when playing in a bunker.

WATER HAZARDS

It is the duty of the club to define clearly the limits of a water hazard, this is usually done by means of yellow stakes or lines marked on the ground. The water level at times may not extend to the stakes or lines set by the club committee, leaving dry or grassy banks between the stakes and the water. This defined area is still a water hazard. If you wish you can play your ball as it lies, but you cannot ground your club or touch the hazard during the address or backswing. The alternative is to drop your ball either under the stroke and distance rule, or for a penalty of one stroke you can drop the ball anywhere behind the hazard, keeping the point where your ball last crossed the line of the hazard between you and the hole.

When dropping the ball make sure you stand so that you are dropping the ball on this line, not to either side.

LATERAL WATER HAZARD

This hazard is water that lies more or less in the direction of the line of play. In most occasions this is a trench for drawing surface water from the fairways. Again the area of the hazard will be defined either with lines on the ground or red stakes.

In this case you can either drop the ball under the water hazard rules, or within two club lengths either side of the hazard, opposite where your ball went into the defined area, under a one-stroke penalty.

THE GREEN

Having started the hole together on the tee, you finish the hole together on the green. It is here that pressure is at its greatest, therefore, good conduct is of great importance. Always look after the surface of the green particularly around the hole. Never take your trolley on to the green; park it at the point where you will exit to the next hole. Equally if you are carrying your bag of clubs, get into the habit of laying them down off the green. Always repair your own pitch marks.

Never walk on the line of another player's putt; if you are asked to attend the flag, stand

A water hazard at the 10th hole at the Belfry.

Opposite: Always repair your own pitch marks on the green.

well clear of the hole, holding the flag at arm's length, making sure the flag will come out easily before the player putts. When replacing the flag avoid marking the rim of the hole. You can mark your ball, lift it and clean it at anytime on the green. This is done by putting a coin or ball marker, into or on the surface behind the ball. If your ball is on the line of another player's putt you might be asked to mark it.

Once you are on the green ensure that you either have someone to attend to the flag or that you take it out of the hole. If you hit the flag when putting in match-play you lose one hole, and in stroke-play it counts as a two-stroke penalty. This rule applies even if the flag is out of the hole lying on the green, so be sure it is not in your line. In match-play if your ball is on the green and your ball strikes your opponent's ball, you lose one hole. In stroke-play you are penalized by two strokes and the balls are played as they lie.

A ball marker.

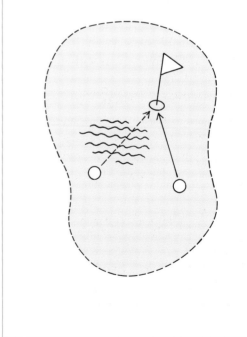

WATER ON THE GREEN

If your ball is in casual water on the green you can claim relief and place the ball clear of the water without penalty. This also applies if water on the green is between you and the hole. The ball must be placed at any point that gives relief but not nearer the hole.

INDEX